IDAHO

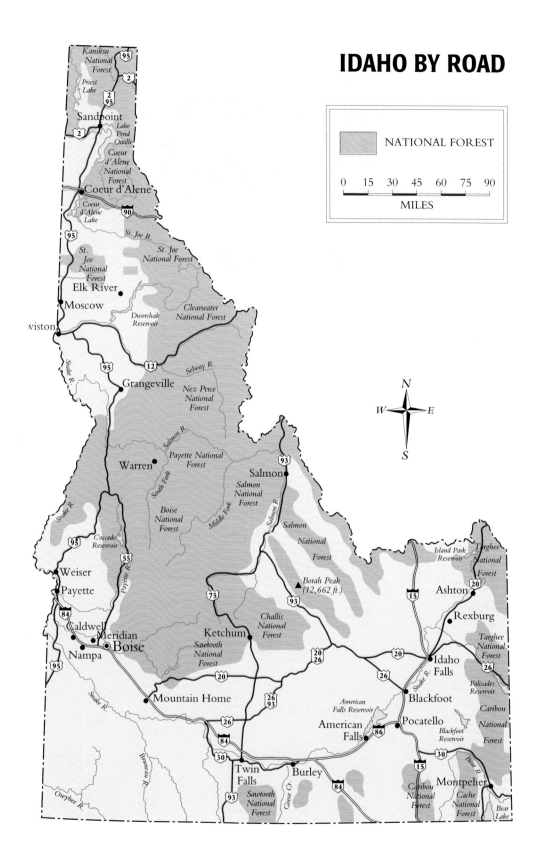

IDAHO BY ROAD

NATIONAL FOREST

MILES
0   15   30   45   60   75   90

N
W — E
S

Kaniksu
National
Forest

Priest
Lake

Sandpoint

Lake
Pend
Oreille

Coeur
d'Alene
National
Forest

Coeur d'Alene

Coeur
d'Alene
Lake

St. Joe R.

St.
Joe
National
Forest

St. Joe
National Forest

Elk River

Moscow

Dworshak
Reservoir

Clearwater
National Forest

Lewiston

Snake R.

Grangeville

Selway R.

Nez Perce
National
Forest

Warren

Salmon R.

Payette National
Forest

South Fork

Boise
National
Forest

Middle Fork

Salmon

Salmon
National
Forest

Salmon R.

Salmon
National
Forest

Borah Peak
(12,662 ft.)

Island Park
Reservoir

Targhee
National
Forest

Ashton

Rexburg

Cascade
Reservoir

Weiser

Payette

Payette R.

Snake R.

Challis
National
Forest

Ketchum

Sawtooth
National
Forest

Caldwell   Meridian
Boise

Nampa

Mountain Home

Snake R.

American
Falls Reservoir

Idaho
Falls

Snake R.

Blackfoot

Targhee
National
Forest

Palisades
Reservoir

Caribou
National
Forest

American
Falls

Pocatello

Blackfoot
Reservoir

Twin
Falls

Burley

Goose Cr.

Bruneau R.

Ouyhee R.

Sawtooth
National
Forest

Caribou
National
Forest

Cache
National
Forest

Montpelier

Bear R.

Bear
Lake

CELEBRATE THE STATES
IDAHO

Rebecca Stefoff

BENCHMARK BOOKS

MARSHALL CAVENDISH
NEW YORK

Benchmark Books
Marshall Cavendish Corporation
99 White Plains Road
Tarrytown, New York 10591-9001

Library of Congress Cataloging-in-Publication Data
Stefoff, Rebecca, date
Idaho / Rebecca Stefoff.
p.   cm.—(Celebrate the states)
Includes bibliographical references and index.
Summary: An introduction to the geography, history, government, economy,
people, achievements, and landmarks of Idaho.
ISBN 0-7614-0663-8 (lib. bdg.)
1. Idaho—Juvenile literature. [1. Idaho.] I. Title. II. Series.
F746.3.S74   2000   979.6—dc21   98-48995   CIP   AC

Maps and graphics supplied by Oxford Cartographers, Oxford, England

Photo research by Candlepants Incorporated

Cover photo: Steve Bly

The photographs in this book are used by permission and through the courtesy of: *Steve Bly*: 6-7, 10-11, 16, 18, 19, 21(top & bottom), 24, 27, 54-55, 62, 64(top), 66, 71, 75, 77, 80(left), 80-81, 81(right), 85, 86, 87, 90-91, 102-103, 107, 110, 114, 122(right). *Photo Researchers Inc.*: David R. Frazier, 15, 64-65, 105; Steve Kraseman, 20; Jeff Lepore, 122(left). *William H. Mullins*: 22, 65, 69, 72-73, 82, 95, 109, 116-117, 119(top & bottom), 125, 127, 137, back cover. *Idaho State Historical Society*: 28-29, 32, #2837 34, #71-204.0 42, #691 46, #64-109.2 50, #73-184.1 52-53, #77-2.45 96. *Joslyn Art Museum, Omaha, Nebraska*: 35. *Buffalo Bill Historical Center, Cody, WY*: 39. *The Church of Jesus Christ Latter Day Saints Archives*: 40. *Historical Photograph Collection, University of Idaho Libraries, Moscow, Idaho*: #5-7-4B, 44; #8-X993, 49; #3-129 5a, 58; Clifford M. Ott Collection, #90-2-24-72b6, 94; A.B. Curtis Collection #13-1952, 97; #3-1761a, 132. *Phil Schermeister*: 60. *C/Z Harris*: 88, 112. *The Image Bank*: Michael Melford, 113. *Corbis*: 133; E.O. Hoppe, 93(top); Bettmann Collection, 93(bottom), 129, 130, 131(right); Jerome Prevost, TempSport, 100; Marc Meunch, 115; Underwood & Underwood, 128; S. Carmona, 131(left).

Printed in Italy

3   5   6   4   2

CONTENTS

INTRODUCTION   IDAHO IS . . .   6

1 GEOGRAPHY   SNOW AND SAGEBRUSH   10
THE SHAPE OF THE LAND • WINTER AND SUMMER • WILD IDAHO • USING LAND
AND WATER

2 HISTORY   INVENTING IDAHO   28
THE INDIANS OF IDAHO • FROM EXPLORATION TO SETTLEMENT • TOWARD
STATEHOOD • SONG: "WAY OUT IN IDAHO" • TWENTIETH-CENTURY IDAHO

3 GOVERNMENT AND ECONOMY   A STATE AT WORK   54
INSIDE GOVERNMENT • FIGHTING FOR CONTROL • GROWING INDUSTRIES •
AGRICULTURE: POTATOES AND MORE • RECIPE: OVEN-ROASTED JO-JOS • TIMBER
AND MINING • CATCHING THE TOURIST DOLLAR

4 PEOPLE   NORTH, SOUTH—AND WEST   72
A STATE WITH THREE CAPITALS • ETHNIC IDAHO • GOING TO EXTREMES? •
AN AMERICAN PARADISE

5 ACHIEVEMENTS   INSPIRING IDAHOANS   90
LITERARY LIFE • BUSINESS AND POLITICS • A MODERN SPORTS HERO

6 LANDMARKS   GEM STATE ROAD TRIP   102
NORTHERN IDAHO • CENTRAL IDAHO • SOUTHERN IDAHO

STATE SURVEY   119
STATE IDENTIFICATIONS • SONG • GEOGRAPHY • TIMELINE • ECONOMY •
CALENDAR OF CELEBRATIONS • STATE STARS • TOUR THE STATE • FUN FACTS

FIND OUT MORE   139

INDEX   142

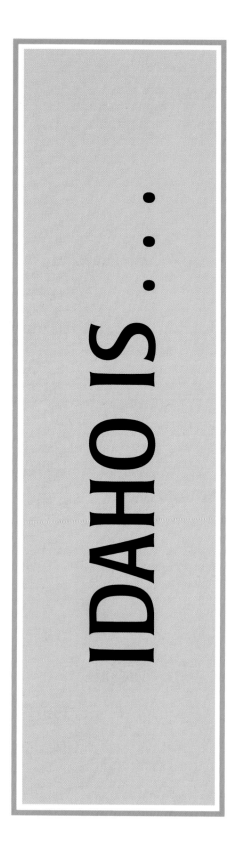

IDAHO IS . . . .

Idaho is something of a mystery to many Americans . . .

"Wedged between six states, in a region so remote that settlers once viewed it more as an obstacle than a destination, is the last frontier of the America that was. The place is Idaho, and although everyone has heard of its potatoes, there seems to be some national confusion over whether Idaho really exists, and if it does, whether it is east or west of the Mississippi."

—David Lamb, *Seattle Times*, 1988

Snooty Boston lady: "Where are you from, my dear?"
Young girl: "Idaho, ma'am."
Lady: "Tut, tut, child. You must learn to pronounce 'Ohio' properly."

—old Idaho joke

. . . but some Idahoans like it that way.

"See what happened when Montana got trendy? People from outside moved in, property taxes went up, and pretty soon regular folks couldn't afford to live there any more. Are we scared of the same thing happening in Idaho? You bet." —Twin Falls resident, 1998

"You're livin' in your own private Idaho,
Underground, like a potato."

—from the song "Your Own Private Idaho" by the B-52s

Idaho's weather and terrain can be harsh . . .

"In fact, I was at one time fearful my feet would freeze in the thin

mockersons [moccasins] which I wore."
—explorer William Clark, 1805, after crossing the Bitterroot Range

"In the raw new land of South Idaho it was shove and scrape, and if you had bad luck or lost your strength you were done for."
—Nancy Stringfellow, describing her 1920s childhood near Twin Falls

. . . but the state has a powerful beauty.

"A lovely, level country spread out for miles and the broad expanse of water lay as a front view, with tall mountains beyond it."
  —Martha Gay Masterson, early settler near Lake Coeur d'Alene

"I live in Colorado, and you know that's a pretty scenic state. But when I have a vacation I come to Idaho. The mountains, the lakes—everything just seems *wilder* here."
  —Jay Lehaskey, a hiker in the Gospel Hump Wilderness

———————————————————

Idaho is a state with an identity crisis. Formed from leftover pieces of other territories, it seems to lack a definite identity of its own. Even its name—a fake "Indian" word—was originally meant for another state. Geography divides Idaho into two distinct regions, and some Idahoans find it easier to identify with their neighbors in nearby states than with the rest of their own state. But divided and ruggedly independent though they may be, Idahoans are united in the proud affection they feel for their state. They are torn between wanting to sing its praises and wanting to keep its secrets to themselves.

1 SNOW AND SAGEBRUSH

To what region of the United States does Idaho belong? As author Sallie Tisdale has pointed out, it isn't easy to tell. She writes, "Because it is stuck between the open land of Washington and Oregon and the Continental Divide of the Rockies, Idaho gets left out. Is it Rocky Mountain country? Perhaps. Is it the Northwest? Perhaps. Is it anything, but Idaho?"

Idaho is a bit of almost everything the West has to offer. It is bounded on the west by the Pacific Northwest states of Washington and Oregon. To the south are the high desert states of Nevada and Utah. On the east are the mountain states of Wyoming and Montana. The Continental Divide, the high, winding track through the Rocky Mountains that separates North America's east-flowing rivers from its west-flowing ones, forms part of Idaho's eastern border. North of Idaho is the Canadian province of British Columbia.

THE SHAPE OF THE LAND

Idaho's shape has been described as a hatchet, a pork chop, and a pregnant letter L. The state's narrow northern section, called the panhandle, is only 45 miles wide at the Canadian border. Idaho is widest at its southern border, which measures 316 miles from east to west. Between these borders is the nation's thirteenth-largest state, almost 84,000 square miles of extremely varied terrain.

LAND AND WATER

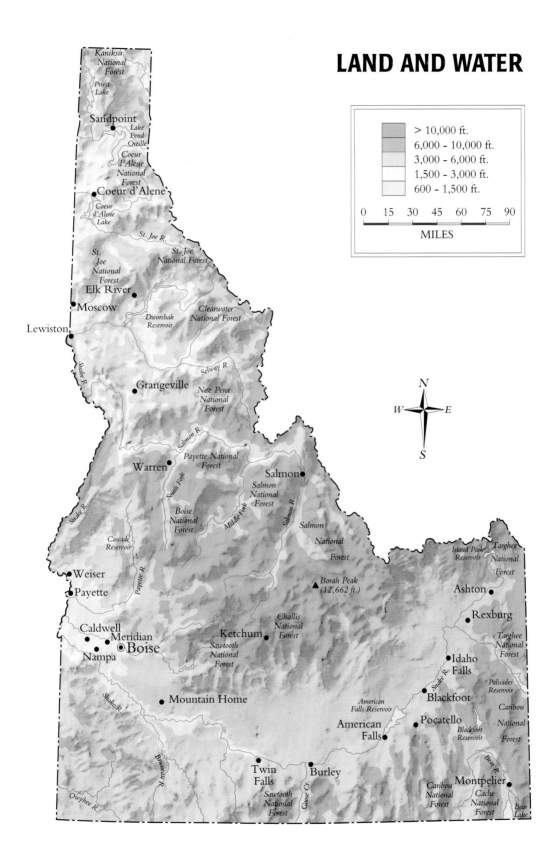

Kaniksu National Forest

Priest Lake

Sandpoint

Lake Pend Oreille

Coeur d'Alene National Forest

Coeur d'Alene

Coeur d'Alene Lake

St. Joe R.

St. Joe National Forest

St. Joe National Forest

Elk River

Moscow

Lewiston

Dworshak Reservoir

Clearwater National Forest

Snake R.

Selway R.

Grangeville

Nez Perce National Forest

Salmon R.

Warren

Payette National Forest

Salmon

Salmon National Forest

South Fork

Middle Fork

Salmon R.

Boise National Forest

Salmon National Forest

Cascade Reservoir

Island Park Reservoir

Targhee National Forest

Snake R.

Payette R.

Weiser

Payette

Borah Peak (12,662 ft.)

Ashton

Rexburg

Caldwell

Meridian

Challis National Forest

Targhee National Forest

Nampa

Boise

Ketchum

Sawtooth National Forest

Idaho Falls

Snake R.

Mountain Home

Palisades Reservoir

Snake R.

Blackfoot

Caribou National Forest

American Falls Reservoir

Pocatello

American Falls

Blackfoot Reservoir

Bruneau R.

Twin Falls

Burley

Goose Cr.

Bear R.

Montpelier

Ouyhee R.

Sawtooth National Forest

Caribou National Forest

Cache National Forest

Bear Lake

Legend

> 10,000 ft.

6,000 – 10,000 ft.

3,000 – 6,000 ft.

1,500 – 3,000 ft.

600 – 1,500 ft.

0 15 30 45 60 75 90

MILES

N

W — E

S

The swift-flowing Salmon River is called the River of No Return because its speed and rapids prevent a canoeist from paddling upstream. The Salmon flows from east to west across the middle of Idaho. Surrounded by steep, tumbled mountain ranges, it divides Idaho into two regions, north and south. Except for a few plateaus, prairies, and meadows, most of Idaho is "one vast sea of mountains," commented one local writer. On a road map, a great many highways and byways in Idaho are labeled "Scenic Drive." It is the twists, turns, and sudden dramatic vistas of the mountain landscape that make them scenic.

Of Idaho's eighty or so mountain ranges, two of the most forbidding are the Bitterroot Range of the Rockies along the eastern border and the jagged Sawtooth Mountains in south-central Idaho. The Selkirk and Coeur d'Alene Ranges dominate the panhandle. Mount Borah, Idaho's highest peak at 12,662 feet, rises from the Lost River Range east of the Sawtooths. The Seven Devils Mountains guard Idaho's western border with Oregon. The Grand Tetons—called by one English traveler in the 1880s "the most perfect example in the world of how mountains should appear on the horizon"—march along its eastern border with Wyoming. The state's southeastern corner has the Caribou Mountains and the Blue Spring Hills.

Between the clustered peaks of south-central Idaho and the southeastern highlands is the Snake River Plain. The Snake River begins in a spring in Wyoming. It enters Idaho and flows west across the southern part of the state in a long, lazy arc. At the Oregon border the Snake plunges into a deep gorge called Hells Canyon before joining the Columbia River, which eventually empties into the Pacific Ocean.

"Few realize that there is such grand scenery in Idaho as that in the Sawtooth," wrote one member of an Idaho women's mountain-climbing club that urged Congress in 1911 to create a national park in the mountains.

The Snake River Plain is the flattest part of Idaho. Over thousands of years the river has carved a deep canyon through the heart of the plain, and in most places the water now flows at the bottom of steep canyon walls or cliffs. Above the river, on the level plain, occasional isolated hills or steep rocky buttes break up the flat landscape.

The southwestern corner of Idaho, far from the river, is much like the neighboring areas of Nevada, Utah, and southeastern Oregon—a high-altitude desert of dry, rolling hills and canyons carved by creeks that often dry up in summer. Rancher Dave Amberson, who grew up in this sternly beautiful part of the state, calls it "a hard place to love, but hard to get out of your blood."

WINTER AND SUMMER

The mountains of central Idaho divide the state into two climate zones. Northern Idaho has a climate like that of Washington and Oregon. Winters are wet and cold, summers warm and dry. Parts of the panhandle receive 96 inches of rain and snow a year—nearly as much as Washington's Olympic Peninsula, famed as one of the nation's wettest places.

Southern Idaho has a climate like that of the Rocky Mountain and Great Plains states. Winters are cold and windy, but drier than those farther north, while summers are hot and dry. Fierce summer thunderstorms sometimes rumble across the plains, bringing towering black clouds from which lightning stabs down at the parched land, igniting wildfires.

"Weather forecasting? Well, that's tricky," admits a park ranger in central Idaho. "Mountains make their own weather systems, and the weather can change in an instant. We get all kinds of extremes.

The Snake River flows through North America's deepest gorge, Hells Canyon, a paradise for hikers, climbers, and white-water rafters.

You can be hiking on a hot July day and get caught in a hailstorm—or a snowstorm." Snow and ice can bring travel to a standstill, especially in central Idaho. Remember those roads marked "Scenic Drive"? Many of them are also marked "May Be Closed in Winter."

Yet snow is vitally important to Idaho. Not only does it thrill skiers, but water from snowmelt feeds the Selway, Lochsa, Clearwater, Coeur d'Alene, Big Lost, and Salmon Rivers, as well as hundreds of smaller waterways. Snowmelt also replenishes Idaho's more than two thousand lakes and waters its forests.

An early settler called Idaho's summer storms "blessed rain and cursed lightning."

Winter can be hard on central and northern Idaho, which sometimes receive heavy snowfalls.

WILD IDAHO

Nearly two-fifths of Idaho is forested. Again, however, there is a big difference between the regions north and south of the Salmon River. More than 80 percent of northern Idaho is covered with forest, compared with less than 30 percent in the south. Evergreens such as Douglas fir, western white pine, and western red cedar flourish in the moist, cool hills and mountains north of the Snake River Plain. The drier south is sagebrush country, an open landscape covered with hardy grasses and shrubs that can withstand heat, cold, and drought. Streams and creeks are lined with stands of birch, aspen, willow, and cottonwood trees whose leaves blaze golden in the fall.

Huge herds of bison once roamed across southern Idaho. Today there are only a few of these shaggy beasts left, mostly on private ranchland. Grizzly bears, black bears, cougars, mountain goats, and bighorn sheep are also less numerous than they once were, but enough remain to make Idaho a wildlife watcher's paradise. There are also moose, elk, white-tailed deer, and pronghorn antelope, as well as beavers, porcupines, wolverines, and prairie dogs. Rock-strewn mountain slopes echo to the whistles of groundhog-like marmots and the shrill "meep, meep" calls of pikas, small, shy rodents that dwell among boulders.

A pika gathers plants that it will dry in the sun and store for the winter.

No other state offers more habitat for Rocky Mountain bighorn sheep.

Wolves were once almost wiped out in Idaho, but during the 1990s the U.S. Forest Service began reintroducing them to some wilderness areas.

THE FATE OF THE WILDERNESS

The federal government owns 64 percent of Idaho. Much of this land is contained within eleven national forests. And within central Idaho's national forests are four million acres of land set aside as wilderness areas under federal protection: the Selway-Bitterroot Wilderness, the Frank Church River of No Return Wilderness, the Gospel Hump Wilderness, and the Sawtooth Wilderness.

Unlike national forests, wilderness areas are protected from such activities as road building, logging, and mining. Conservationists argue that such protection is necessary to preserve Idaho's natural heritage, both for the health of the land itself and for the enjoyment of future generations. Yet many Idahoans disagree with the conservationist viewpoint. In a state where large numbers of people have traditionally made their living from industries such as logging and mining, many feel that locking up large tracts of backcountry land as protected wilderness costs the state jobs and money.

In 1989 Steve Symms, a U.S. senator from Idaho, called the wilderness issue "a political hot potato"—something extremely difficult to handle. That is still true. The conflict between those who want to save Idaho's wilderness and those who want to use it is one of the core issues of Idaho political life.

More than 350 species of birds have been sighted in Idaho. Some live there year-round, while others pass through during migration. Waterbirds such as herons, geese, and ducks are plentiful around lakes and rivers. Smaller species that live in meadows and prairies include hummingbirds, meadowlarks, and mountain bluebirds, the state bird.

Idaho is especially rich in birds of prey—hawks, falcons, and eagles. The Snake River Birds of Prey Natural Area near the town of Kuna in southern Idaho has the nation's largest concentration of these birds. They nest in the rocky canyon walls and soar forth on widespread wings to scan Idaho's rugged landscape with their keen hunters' eyes.

USING LAND AND WATER

Much of Idaho is too mountainous for farming. The Snake River Plain, however, is flat and covered with fertile volcanic soil. Without the help of the Snake River, which provides a constant supply of water for irrigation, it would be much too dry for agriculture. Of the total irrigated farmland in the United States, nearly a tenth is in Idaho.

The Snake River Plain's combination of level land and steady water supply has made it Idaho's center of settlement and urban growth. Half of all Idahoans live within fifty miles of the river's banks. The state's five largest cities—Boise, Pocatello, Idaho Falls, Nampa, and Twin Falls—are located on or near the river. In contrast, some counties in central Idaho do not even have one person per square mile.

People have changed the face of Idaho, especially in the south, where plowed fields, orchards, and the fencelines of ranches draw straight lines across the rolling landscape. Above all, people have changed the rivers. Once the Snake River's 570-mile course through Idaho was a series of turbulent waterfalls and churning rapids as the mighty Snake dropped more than six thousand feet from its source high in the mountains to where it meets the Columbia. Today several dozen dams tame the river's flow and turn long stretches of it into sluggish, slow-moving reservoirs.

The dams have played a vital role in Idaho's development. They provide water for irrigation and hydroelectric power for industries and homes. Yet progress always comes at a price, and in Idaho it

The sister cities of Lewiston, Idaho, and Clarkston, Washington—named for explorers Lewis and Clark—face each other across the Snake River.

is salmon that have paid the price. Once Idaho's rivers teemed with these fish, which spend part of their lives in the ocean but migrate far up freshwater streams to breed. But each new dam made it harder for fish to struggle upstream past concrete barriers to their spawning grounds, and harder for young salmon to swim downstream to the sea. Today there are few salmon in Idaho rivers—even in the Salmon River.

In the late 1990s, the U.S. Army Corps of Engineers, which owns and operates four dams on the lower Snake River, announced that it was studying the possibility of removing the dams to increase the number of salmon that make it to Idaho. The suggestion aroused outrage in the city of Lewiston on the Snake River. Many people claim that the local economy depends upon cheap electricity and river shipping, which the dams make possible. A port official in Lewiston called the idea of eliminating the dams "crazy" and "out of left field." Yet between 1984 and 1998 government agencies in the Snake River region spent $3 billion on fish ladders, hatcheries, and other programs to help improve conditions for the salmon—with no results. The plight of the salmon shows that there are no easy answers to Idaho's environmental problems.

Pollution has also been a problem for Idahoans. In the mid-1980s the sparkling blue waters of Lake Coeur d'Alene were found to be contaminated with one of the highest levels of lead in the United States. The lead, along with other dangerous materials, had

The Boise River offers a cool escape from summer heat.

flowed downstream for years from mining operations on the Coeur d'Alene River. Another dangerously polluted region is Silver Valley in northern Idaho, the largest silver-producing area in the world. Here, mineral refineries sent chemicals into the air and water.

Since those days Idaho has made great strides toward reducing pollution, largely because of stricter laws limiting the amount of harmful substances that businesses can discharge into the air and water. The Boise River, once badly damaged by waste from sawmills and meatpacking plants, is now so clean you can safely float down it on an inner tube. Many polluted sites remain to be cleaned up, however, and Idahoans must stay alert if they are to protect their land, air, and water from new sources of pollution.

2 INVENTING IDAHO

Seven Devils Mountains, by Edward Smith

SUMMER READING CHALLENGE

SHOW US HOW YOU

PRESS PLAY!

DURING NPL'S SUMMER READING CHALLENGE

MAY 3 - AUGUST 21

Register on our website to start reading, learning, and earning points for free prizes!

library.nashville.org/summerchallenge

Idaho is new. Of the lands that would become the fifty United States, Idaho was the last to be entered by white people. It did not become a state until 1890. But Idaho's human history stretches far into the past and weaves together the stories of many different kinds of people.

THE INDIANS OF IDAHO

People first appeared in Idaho about 12,000 years ago—perhaps even earlier. They were descended from wandering hunters who had crossed into present-day Alaska from Asia and then spread out across North America. These people are known to us only through a few remains such as scattered bones and traces of old hunting camps, but they were the ancestors of the Native Americans who have lived in Idaho for more than a thousand years.

Many different Native American groups lived in Idaho. The Kutenai, Coeur d'Alene, and Kalispell lived in northern Idaho. North-central Idaho, between the Clearwater and Salmon Rivers, was part of the homeland of the Nez Perces. The Shoshones lived in the high desert sagebrush country of southern Idaho. Mingled with the Shoshones were a closely related group called the Bannocks. Another related group, the Northern Paiutes, lived in southeastern Oregon and southwestern Idaho.

All of these tribes lived in small family groups or bands and spent much of the year moving about in search of food. In summer they built pole lodges covered with reed mats. They spent the winters in circular houses built partly underground for warmth. The Shoshones' resources included the salmon that were then abundant in Idaho's rivers, the bison that roamed the southern plains, and the camas bulb, a plant similar to an onion. The Northern Paiutes scoured their arid territory for pine nuts, birds, and small game such as rabbits. The northern tribes lived primarily by fishing for salmon, which they caught in May and June and then dried for use throughout the year.

Around 1700, the Shoshones obtained horses from Indians farther south. Horses allowed them to travel east to the Great Plains to hunt bison and to trade with the tribes there, who were beginning to possess European trade items. The Shoshones were one of the last tribes in the region to acquire firearms, however. Their neighbors to the east and south—the Arapaho, Blackfoot, Cheyenne, and Ute Indians—obtained guns and began attacking the Shoshones, trying to drive them back into the mountains of Idaho.

Like the Shoshones, the Nez Perces acquired horses in the early 1700s. They quickly became skilled riders, traveling to the Great Plains to hunt and trade. The Nez Perces borrowed some customs, such as making buffalo-skin tepees, from the Plains Indians. And in the rolling, hilly district called the Palouse, in northwestern Idaho and eastern Washington, they bred a type of strong, spotted horse now known as an Appaloosa.

The Nez Perces and the Shoshones were bitter enemies who frequently warred against one another, but they usually stopped

The Indians of Idaho became expert horsemen, a skill that Charles Ostner captured in this 1865 painting called Bear Attack.

fighting in summertime. They even did business with one another at the annual Indian rendezvous. This gathering of many tribes took place each year near the site of the present-day town of Weiser, Idaho. For a month or two Native Americans from all directions traded, gambled, and danced together peacefully. The rendezvous, which continued into the 1860s, was a major event in the lives of the Idaho Indians.

IRON-MAN: A SHOSHONE TALE

This Shoshone story shows how some Indians wove the newly arrived Euro-Americans into their tales and legends:

Iron-Man, the father of the white people, lived on the water. Wolf, the father of the Indians, lived underground. One day Iron-Man invited Wolf to visit. Iron-Man gave his pipe to Wolf, who smoked up all of the tobacco. Then the father of the Indians took his little pipe from his quiver and handed it to Iron-Man. The father of the white men smoked until the house was full of smoke, but he could not smoke up all of the tobacco in the pipe. Wolf's son told his father that Iron-Man was nearly dead, so Wolf made the smoke disappear and made Iron-Man well again. Then Iron-Man brought a large iron ball and gave half to his friend. "We are now going to make guns," he said. Both made guns as quickly as possible. Wolf made more guns in the same time than Iron-Man. That is how the father of the Indians won that contest.

In this tale, the Indians defeated the whites in a contest involving guns. Perhaps it reveals the Indians' wish that they *could* make guns, for in the end they lost the biggest contest of all to the superior force of the whites.

FROM EXPLORATION TO SETTLEMENT

The first Euro-Americans to arrive in Idaho were explorers on a mission for the United States. Some of those who followed came in search of furs, and some came to preach and teach. It was many years, however, before the first settlers came to Idaho to stay.

The Explorers. From May 1804 to September 1806, Meriwether Lewis and William Clark led a small expedition called the Corps of Discovery west from St. Louis on the Missouri River to the mouth of the Columbia River on the Pacific Ocean—and back again. They were the first white Americans to cross the West. Although they encountered many hardships during the journey, crossing Idaho was the worst part.

In August 1805, the Lewis and Clark expedition crossed the Con-

The Lewis and Clark expedition camped with Native Americans on its journey through the West.

tinental Divide at Lemhi Pass and stood at the edge of Idaho. Ahead of them stretched a wilderness of savage peaks, a landscape too difficult to cross. They struggled north to Lolo Pass and tried again to head west, only to become lost and snowbound in what expedition member Patrick Gass called "this horrible mountainous desert." Food was in such short supply that they dined on bear oil and candles. Finally they made contact with friendly Nez Perces who fed the explorers and guided the expedition out of the Bitterroots. When Lewis and Clark returned to St. Louis the following year, they spoke enthusiastically of the wonders of the West, but they had little good to say about the torturous terrain and difficult conditions of what would become Idaho.

Mountain Men and Missionaries. Europe's passion for fur hats and coats sent trappers and traders far into the American West in search of beaver pelts. Soon after the return of the Corps of Discovery, a British firm called the North West Company, based in Montreal, Canada, sent its agent David Thompson to set up a fur trade in the region Lewis and Clark had explored. In 1809, Thompson established a trading post called Kullyspell House on the shores of Lake Pend Oreille. This, the first non-Indian structure in Idaho, lasted for about two years. Beginning in 1818, British trappers from Canada descended into Idaho each year in what were called the Snake River brigades. The brigades reaped thousands of valuable beaver pelts, but hostile Indians and rough terrain made their ventures so dangerous that one trapper vowed he would return only when the beaver had skins of gold.

The Americans were not about to let the British get all the furs in the northern Rockies. Andrew Henry of St. Louis led a party of

Mountain men prepare a beaver trap. The stick is bait to lure the animal into the trap hidden beneath it.

American trappers into Idaho in 1810. Gradually, more American trappers trekked into the area. These hardy adventurers came to be called mountain men. Some of them, including Jim Bridger and John Colter, were among the foremost explorers of the western mountains. Between 1825 and 1840, they and several hundred other trappers met each summer at a rowdy gathering to drink, gamble, and sell their furs to traders from back east. One such trader, Nathaniel Wyeth of Boston, founded a permanent trading post near present-day Pocatello in 1834. He named it Fort Hall, and it became a major outpost in the Snake River country.

The glory days of the fur trade were over by 1850. By then a new wave of outsiders had begun coming to Idaho, not to obtain furs but to guide the Native Americans toward Christianity and Euro-American civilization.

The first Protestant missionaries in Idaho were Henry and Eliza Spalding, who traveled west in 1836 with another missionary couple, the Whitmans. The Whitmans established a mission in eastern Washington, while the Spaldings set themselves up at Lapwai in western Idaho. A few years later another missionary couple established a mission near Kamiah. These missions were hastily abandoned after a tragic incident in which Indians, angered by an outbreak of disease introduced by white newcomers, killed the Whitmans and other whites in Washington. This first Protestant missionary effort accomplished little in its eleven-year existence—only twenty-one Indians converted to Christianity.

The Roman Catholic Church also sent missionaries into Idaho and the Pacific Northwest. One of the first, Pierre Jean De Smet, founded a mission among the Coeur d'Alene Indians. The Catholics proved more successful than the Protestants had been— within a few generations, two-thirds of the Coeur d'Alene tribe had joined the Catholic church. The Sacred Heart Mission in Cataldo, a church built in the late 1840s by Catholic missionaries and their converts, is the oldest surviving building in Idaho.

Pioneers and Settlers. The mountain men and the missionaries opened the way for overland travel across the northern Rockies. Land-hungry Americans east of the Mississippi River were eager to settle in the fertile, hospitable lands that Lewis and Clark had discovered in the Oregon country west of Idaho. In the early 1840s, a great migration began, as thousands of people walked the Oregon Trail to new homes. The Oregon Trail was a two-thousand-mile, six-month journey across prairies and rivers, over mountains, and through deserts. Between 1840 and 1860 about 53,000 men, women, and children traveled the trail. Some were bound for Oregon, others for California. None of them lingered in Idaho. Indeed, they considered their passage through the Snake River Plain to be one of the worst parts of the trip. They usually reached Idaho in late summer, when the blistering heat was at its worst. They and their pack animals were weary and footsore. Food was often beginning to run short. Worst of all, water glimmered tantalizingly at the bottom of the Snake River canyon, but in many places the canyon walls were so steep and dangerous that the thirsty travelers could not get to the water. "If once we are brought safe through this hard place," Sarah Rodgers wrote in her journal while passing through Idaho, "surely we shall never return."

Pioneers on the Oregon Trail were happy to refresh themselves and renew their supplies at Fort Hall and Fort Boise. But they did not look at Idaho as a possible site for settlement—only as an obstacle to be overcome on their way to the good lands farther west. Those who finally established the first settlement in Idaho came from the south. A religious group called the Church of Jesus Christ of Latter-Day Saints—also known as the Mormons—had fled from the East to the desolate wilds of Utah to escape persecu-

Nathaniel Wyeth raised a homemade American flag over Fort Hall on August 6, 1834. Later the fort provided supplies to thousands of travelers along the Oregon Trail.

tion for their unusual beliefs. Not only did the Mormons claim that the founder of their sect was a holy prophet, they allowed men to have more than one wife—a practice that most Americans found shocking.

The Mormons built a flourishing colony in northern Utah and soon attempted to establish a satellite colony to the north. In 1855, they founded a short-lived settlement called Lemhi in Idaho. It failed, but in 1860 the Mormons tried again. Twenty-three families established the town of Franklin, Idaho's first permanent settlement. Soon other Mormon communities had taken root in southern Idaho.

But Idaho was not yet called Idaho. It was part of the Oregon Territory until 1853, when Congress split the region and created Washington Territory north of the Columbia River. Now the future Idaho was divided between Oregon and Washington Territories. When Oregon became a state in 1859, all of Idaho became part of Washington Territory.

Mormon families from Utah established the first permanent white settlements in southeastern Idaho.

TOWARD STATEHOOD

In 1860, the year Mormons founded Franklin, prospectors discovered gold in the Clearwater River region of central Idaho. The gold rush brought thousands of miners from Oregon, California, and the East, eager to make their fortunes. After them came merchants, traders, thieves, saloon operators, gamblers, and dance-hall women, eager to take the gold away from the miners. Soon boomtowns such as Orofino, Lewiston, and Florence sprang up in the wild land. Gold strikes to the south, along the Boise River, gave birth to Idaho City and other mining towns. Already Idaho was becoming a place of contrasts and divisions. The rough-and-tumble, lawless mining camps could not have been more different from the orderly, law-abiding Mormon towns.

The government of Washington Territory was located in Olympia, far away from Idaho, and the politicians there found Idaho troublesome and hard to govern. They asked the U.S. Congress to take it off their hands, and in 1863 Congress created the Idaho Territory, which included not only Idaho but also parts of Montana and Wyoming. Soon Congress trimmed eastern portions of Idaho away, giving them to other new territories. By 1868, Idaho had acquired its present borders.

Congress chose the name Idaho Territory because one of the steamboats that carried miners up the Columbia River to Lewiston was called the *Idaho*. The name had been suggested by a miner a few years earlier as a possible name for Colorado. He claimed that *Idaho* meant "gem of the mountains" in an Indian language, but in fact it means nothing at all—he had simply made it up. Congress did not

WAY OUT IN IDAHO

The Oregon Short Line was completed in 1884. It ran from Pocatello through the Snake River valley. The building of this and other railroads opened up the Idaho Territory and helped the lead and silver mining industries.

I was roaming around in Denver one luckless rainy day,
When Kilpatrick's man, Catcher, stepped up to me and did say,
"I'll lay you down five dollars as quickly as I can,
And you'll hurry up and catch the train, she's starting for Cheyenne." *Chorus*

He laid me down five dollars, like many another man,
And I started for the depot as happy as a clam;
When I got to Pocatello, my troubles began to grow,
A-wading though the sagebrush in frost and rain and snow. *Chorus*

When I got to American Falls, it was there I met Fat Jack.
He said he kept a hotel in a dirty canvas shack.
"We hear you are a stranger and perhaps your funds are low.
Well, yonder stands my hotel tent, the best in Idaho." *Chorus*

I followed my conductor into his hotel tent,
And for one square and hearty meal I paid him my last cent;
But Jack's a jolly fellow, and you'll always find him so,
A-workin' on the narrow-gauge way out in Idaho. *Chorus*

They put me to work next morning with a cranky cuss called Bill,
And they gave me a ten-pound hammer to strike upon a drill.
They said if I didn't like it I could take my shirt and go,
And they'd keep my blanket for my board way out in Idaho. *Chorus*

It filled my heart with pity as I walked along the track
To see so many old bummers with their turkeys on their backs.
They said the work was heavy and the grub they couldn't go.
Around Kilpatrick's tables way out in Idaho. *Chorus*

But now I'm well and happy, down in the harvest camps,
And there I will continue till I make a few more stamps.
I'll go down to New Mexico and I'll marry the girl I know,
And I'll buy me a horse and buggy and go back to Idaho. *Chorus*

Gold miners tried to drown their sorrows in saloons such as this one in Lewiston, which dates from the 1860s.

know that in 1863, however, and the popular name became attached to the new territory.

"Idaho's early territorial years can only be described as a time of trouble," writes historian Carlos A. Schwantes. In 1864, when the territory's administrators decided to move the capital from Lewiston to Boise, the people of Lewiston rebelled and placed the territorial seal under armed guard. Citizens from Boise tried to steal it. Eventually the capital did move, but the unforgiving people of

Lewiston repeatedly tried to have their part of Idaho rejoined to Washington. The poor performance of Idaho's territorial governors also caused problems. The territory had sixteen governors in twenty-seven years. Four failed to take office. Six spent less than a year—sometimes only a few days—in Idaho. Government officials also stole large sums from the territorial treasury.

These administrative troubles, however, were nothing compared to the turmoil faced by Idaho's Native Americans. They suffered terribly from new diseases introduced by the whites, and the inrush of miners, settlers, and livestock occupied more and more of the land that the Indians needed to support their traditional way of life. U.S. Army and government officials began forcing the Indians onto reservations.

Then, in 1863, tragedy struck southeastern Idaho. Starving Shoshone-Bannock Indians had been raiding wagon trains and the town of Franklin. A group of California volunteers marched into the region and attacked a Shoshone band at Bear River. Twenty-two Californians died. The death toll among the Indians was far higher. Utah settlers visited the battlefield and counted 368 dead Indians, including nearly 90 women and children. After this disaster, the Shoshone-Bannock agreed to move onto the Fort Hall Reservation.

The Nez Perces met a similar fate in 1877. Some Nez Perces had moved onto the Clearwater Reservation, but others claimed the right to live in their traditional homeland, the Wallowa Valley of northeastern Oregon. Settlers wanted the valley, however, so the federal government told the army to move the Nez Perces to Idaho. A fight broke out, and eight hundred Indians, led by Chief Joseph, fled through the winter snows toward Canada. The pursuing soldiers caught up with them in Montana. Chief Joseph is supposed to have declared, "My heart is sick and sad. From where the sun now stands I will fight no more forever." Some of the Nez Perces eventually ended up in Idaho, although Chief Joseph lived out his days on a reservation in Washington.

Idaho's last Indian uprisings occurred in the late 1870s as Native Americans in southern Idaho struggled in vain to hold back the rising tide of settlers. Soon all of Idaho's Indians were confined to reservations. In the coming years, the government repeatedly cut these reservations down in size to please the incoming white

Chief Joseph, whose Indian name was Hin-mah-too-yah-lat-kekht ("Thunder Traveling to Loftier Mountain Heights"). He led his people through the Bitterroot Mountains but could not save them from the U.S. Army.

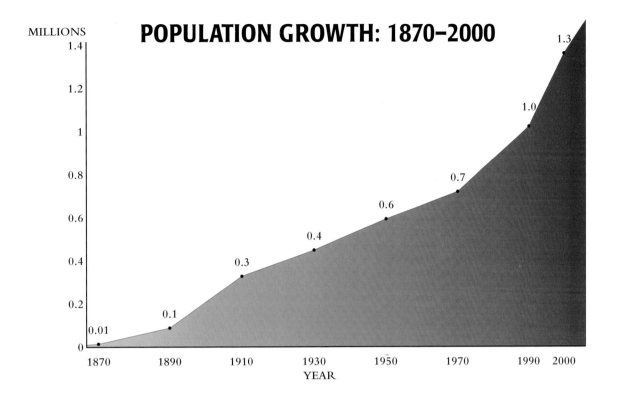

POPULATION GROWTH: 1870–2000

MILLIONS

1.3

1.0

0.7

0.6

0.4

0.3

0.1

0.01

YEAR

settlers, ranchers, and miners who demanded more and more of Idaho for their own.

By the late 1880s, the Idaho Territory had about 90,000 residents. They were clamoring for statehood—although they did not all want to be in the *same* state. Some in the north wanted to join Washington State, created in 1889. Congress came close to dividing the Idaho Territory between Washington and Nevada, but the people of southern Idaho were horrified by the idea of becoming part of Nevada, which had a reputation for crooked politics. The territory's governor convinced President Grover Cleveland that

Idaho should remain united, and in 1890 Congress made Idaho the nation's forty-third state.

TWENTIETH-CENTURY IDAHO

During its first years of statehood Idaho was plagued by labor struggles, as miners fought to improve their wages and working conditions. The miners formed organizations called unions, which sometimes went out on strike, refusing to work until their demands were met. Clashes between striking mine workers and stubborn mine owners frequently flared into violence. In 1892, striking miners in the Coeur d'Alene region dynamited a mill, killing six people. Then, in 1899, the union attacked a mining company that had refused to hire union workers, blowing the company's offices to bits. Federal troops arrested hundreds of miners. A few years later an assassin killed Governor Frank Steunenberg and claimed that union officials had hired him. The officials were found not guilty in a sensational 1907 trial, and the era of Idaho's worst mining wars drew to an end.

By this time, new industries were developing. In the early 1900s, timber companies started buying and logging large tracts of Idaho land. Despite raging forest fires in 1910 that consumed three million acres of trees, the timber industry steadily grew in importance. Agriculture also grew. As early as the days of Henry Spalding's Lapwai mission, farmers had found that potatoes grew well in Idaho's sandy soil. By 1929, the state was producing 25 million bushels of spuds a year.

The worldwide economic depression of the 1930s caused great

Miners at the entrance to a mine they called the Mother Lode, near Murray,
around 1885.

misery in Idaho. As the price of minerals, timber, and farm produce
dropped, Idahoans' incomes also plummeted. Some people grew
so desperate that they began setting fires so that they could earn a
few dollars by serving on the emergency crews that put the fires
out.

In the midst of the depression, however, one sign of a bright new
future appeared on the horizon. A railroad executive who wanted to

The potato-based businesses along this Idaho Falls street earned it the nickname Spud Alley.

develop a European-style ski resort in the United States chose a site near the old Idaho mining town of Ketchum. The railroad poured development money into the place, and the luxury resort of Sun Valley was born in 1938. It was a hint of the coming boom in outdoor sports and the rise of tourism.

An entirely different kind of camp rose in 1942 at Minidoka, north of Twin Falls. It was one of many relocation centers for Japanese Americans from the West Coast during World War II. Driven by the suspicion that people of Japanese descent would aid Japan, America's enemy in the war, the federal government overrode their civil rights and placed them in camps such as Minidoka. Nearly 10,000 Japanese Americans were confined at Minidoka, where they lived in barracks covered in tar paper and surrounded by barbed wire. The 1,200 Japanese Americans who had been living in Idaho

TEN LARGEST CITIES

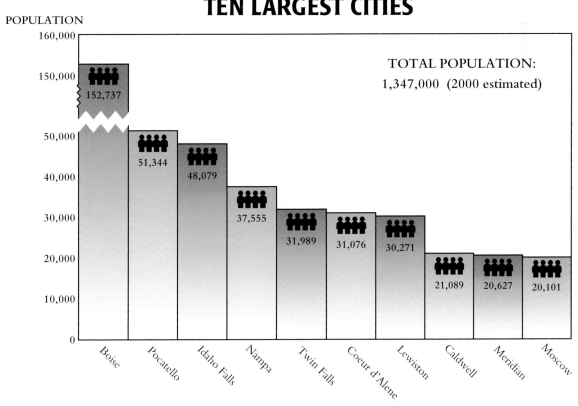

POPULATION

TOTAL POPULATION: 1,347,000 (2000 estimated)

Boise 152,737
Pocatello 51,344
Idaho Falls 48,079
Nampa 37,555
Twin Falls 31,989
Coeur d'Alene 31,076
Lewiston 30,271
Caldwell 21,089
Meridian 20,627
Moscow 20,101

at the outbreak of the war were not put into the camps, although they did suffer from anti-Japanese prejudice. After the war ended in 1945, some of the relocated people from the West Coast stayed in Idaho, enlarging the Japanese-American community there.

Idaho contributed a milestone to history in 1951, when a power plant at a research center now called the Idaho National Engineering and Environmental Laboratory (INEEL) became the first place in the world to produce electricity from atomic energy. The nearby town of Arco still proudly boasts that it was the first town lit by nuclear power. Again, however, progress came at a price. By the late 1980s, nuclear waste had made INEEL one of the nation's most dangerously contaminated sites.

Camp Minidoka, north of Twin Falls. Taken from their homes in the Seattle area, thousands of Japanese Americans waited out World War II in the camp.

Modern Idaho reflects the trends that have met and mingled in the state during the second half of the 1900s. A rush of dam building led to plentiful electricity and more irrigation—but also drew criticism from the growing environmental movement after the 1970s. Wilderness has attracted ever-growing numbers of admiring visitors and tourist dollars—but timber and mining companies also want to claim their piece of it. People from outside are moving into Idaho. Some work in new, high-technology firms in Boise or other fast-growing cities. Others hope to return to the pioneer lifestyle in small rural towns or on isolated homesteads. As Idaho moves into its second century of statehood, it remains a jumble of contradictions.

3 A STATE AT WORK

The state capitol in Boise

Before it could become a state, Idaho needed a constitution to serve as the basis of law and government. Idaho's constitution has changed a lot since the people of the territory created it in 1889. It represents Idahoans' best effort to set forth rules and values upon which all can agree.

INSIDE GOVERNMENT

Like the federal government, the Idaho state government is divided into three branches.

Executive. The head of the executive branch of government is the governor. His or her principal responsibility is overseeing the smooth running of all of the departments and agencies that administer laws and do the state's work. The governor also works with state legislators in the lawmaking process and represents Idaho at the national level by communicating the state's needs to the president. Idaho voters elect the governor to a term of four years.

Idaho has had some noteworthy governors. Moses Alexander, who served from 1915 to 1919, was the first Jewish governor in the United States. Cecil Andrus served four terms as governor in the 1970s, 1980s, and 1990s and also figured in national government. As governor he fought to control the mining industry and established the Sawtooth and Hells Canyon National Recreation Areas.

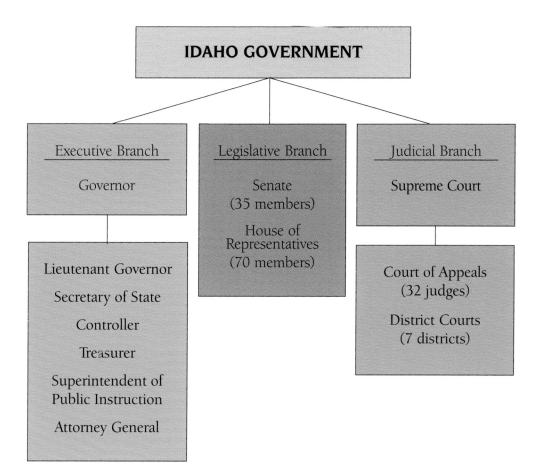

IDAHO GOVERNMENT

Executive Branch

Governor

Lieutenant Governor

Secretary of State

Controller

Treasurer

Superintendent of
Public Instruction

Attorney General

Legislative Branch

Senate
(35 members)

House of
Representatives
(70 members)

Judicial Branch

Supreme Court

Court of Appeals
(32 judges)

District Courts
(7 districts)

As U.S. secretary of the interior from 1977 to 1981, he helped protect wilderness land in Alaska.

Other important elected officials of the executive branch are the lieutenant governor, the secretary of state, the state controller, the state treasurer, the attorney general, and the superintendent of public instruction. They are responsible for overseeing the departments of government that carry out Idaho's laws. Because Idaho contains a greater percentage of federally owned land than any state except Alaska, Idaho's state officials must work frequently and closely with federal officials and agencies. The controller pays the

Cecil Andrus, a logger who became a politician, declared, "The most important long-range issue is the protection of our magnificent Idaho environment."

state's bills, and the treasurer keeps track of and invests the state's money.

Legislative. The legislative branch makes laws for the state. It consists of two bodies, the senate and the house of representatives. Thirty-five elected senators and seventy elected representatives serve two-year terms. Members of the legislature form committees to develop laws dealing with such matters as education, finance, the environment, health and welfare, transportation, defense, local government, and agricultural affairs.

The legislature introduces and votes on bills, which are proposals involving laws or the spending of public funds. Both the senate and the house of representatives must vote to pass a bill. The bill becomes law when the governor signs it. Even if the governor doesn't sign it, a bill can become law if two-thirds of the lawmakers in each body of the legislature approve it.

Judicial. The judicial branch of government is responsible for interpreting the law. The first level of the judicial system consists of general district courts. The district court judges, elected to four-year terms, hear civil and criminal cases. Their decisions may be appealed in the court of appeals, which consists of three elected judges who serve six-year terms. The state's highest court is the Idaho Supreme Court, which hears cases referred from the court of appeals and also decides cases related to the state constitution. The five supreme court justices are elected to six-year terms.

FIGHTING FOR CONTROL

One of Idaho's hot political issues in the late 1990s centered on the Nez Perce Reservation east of Lewiston. It brought the 3,000 members of the Nez Perce tribe into conflict with the nearly 14,000 non-Indian Idahoans who live and work within the reservation, which was opened to white homesteading in 1893 and now contains several towns. Nearly 90 percent of the reservation now belongs to non-Indians or to government agencies.

The tribe claims the right to control reservation land and has asked for a greater percentage of Indians to be employed on public projects on the reservation. Non-Indian residents and town officials have countered that the old reservation boundaries no longer apply and that they do not have to follow tribal codes and

Conflicts between the Nez Perce and white Idahoans over control of the land on the Nez Perce Reservation has become common in recent years.

laws, such as decisions about land use and ownership, that the Nez Perce have created. Jaime Pinkham, an elected official of the tribe, called this response "the most serious threat [the Nez Perce] community has faced in my lifetime." The tribe warned that if its claim to control of the reservation is not honored it could cancel the rights-of-way for the roads and the gas, electric, telephone, and water lines that cross the reservation and provide necessary services to north-central Idaho.

"As far as I'm concerned," said one frustrated non-Indian resident, "the reservation should be no more." Tribal spokesperson Sam Penney declared, "We are a responsible government" and said that the Nez Perces hoped to settle the dispute over who really owns the reservation through conversations with their non-Indian neighbors, not through lawsuits. Both sides, however, realize that agreeing on who controls what will be a long, difficult process. Meanwhile, tribes elsewhere in Idaho and throughout the West are paying close attention to events at the Nez Perce Reservation, which may set a pattern for handling similar conflicts on other Indian lands.

GROWING INDUSTRIES

Idahoans like to think of themselves as living off the land. The truth is, however, that a growing number of them earn their living in

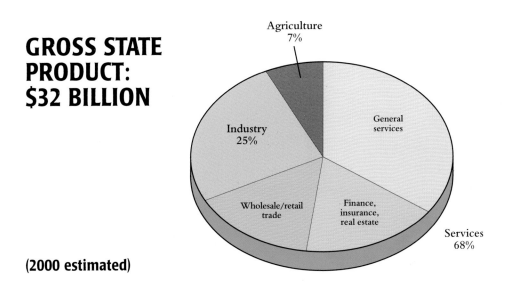

GROSS STATE PRODUCT: $32 BILLION

Agriculture 7%

General services

Industry 25%

Wholesale/retail trade

Finance, insurance, real estate

Services 68%

(2000 estimated)

offices and factories. In terms of the amount of money earned, Idaho's top economic activity is manufacturing—everything from construction equipment to high-technology electronic components such as computer chips and laser printers. Engineering and research are also booming in Idaho. While many Idahoans work for private high-tech firms, government-run INEEL employs three thousand scientists and engineers.

Yet the land and what it produces are still vital to Idaho's economic health. Although farming, forestry, fishing, and mining combined employ little more than one-tenth of the state's workers, these industries contribute significant portions of the state's income.

AGRICULTURE: POTATOES AND MORE

Agriculture accounts for the second-largest portion of Idaho's income. And closely related is the state's fourth-largest industry,

High-technology manufacturing is a growing part of Idaho's economy.

food processing—the canning, freezing, and packaging of food. For many people around the nation and the world, Idaho *is* agriculture. More specifically, it is the potato. Over the years the state has exported millions of bags of spuds, all proudly labeled "Idaho Grown." Even Idaho's license plate promotes the humble tuber through the slogan "Famous Potatoes."

A third of all the potatoes grown in the United States come from Idaho. Most are grown in the Snake River Plain. During harvesttime everyone pitches in to bring in the crop. Each fall, ten of the state's school districts give children time off to help with the potato harvest on their family farms. "I like doing it," says an eleven-year-old as he sorts spuds in the cellar of his uncle's barn. "I might want to have my own farm someday, so this is good experience. Besides, it's more fun than being in school. This afternoon I'm going out in the fields on the trucks."

The future of the potato looks good—the average American eats about 138 pounds of spuds a year (including chips and fries). But the famous potato is not Idaho's only crop. Farmers in forty-two of the state's forty-four counties grow wheat. The state's annual wheat production would fill a train stretching the 340 miles from Boise to Salt Lake City. Peas, lentils, sugar beets, and plums are other leading crops. And Idaho ranks third in the nation as a producer of onions, barley, mint, and hops (a plant used in beer making).

Livestock ranching accounts for about a third of Idaho's agricultural income. The state's land and climate are well suited to sheep, but Idahoans also raise both beef and dairy cattle. Several large hatcheries in Idaho produce trout to stock the state's rivers and to

Idaho is the country's third-ranking producer of onions. Like the potatoes that become french fries, many of Idaho's onions are destined for fast-food restaurants.

A Basque sheepherder at work during lambing season. Basque people settled in Oregon and Nevada, too, but Idaho has the country's greatest concentration of them.

The potato harvest is the big event of the year for farmers in the Snake River Plain.

OVEN-ROASTED JO-JOS

Jo-jos are roasted potato chunks—something like french fries but bigger, better, and a lot less greasy. Of course, the best way to make them is with a couple of large, firm Idaho spuds. Have an adult help you make your jo-jos.

Preheat your oven to 400 degrees.

Scrub your potatoes well with a vegetable brush, leaving the skins on, and then pat them dry with a paper towel. Slice each potato in two lengthwise. Then slice each half lengthwise into two or three wedges, depending upon the size of the spud.

Put a very small amount of vegetable oil—no more than a teaspoonful for up to four large potatoes—into a plastic bag. Put the potato wedges into the bag and shake well so that each wedge has a light, thin coating of oil.

Spread the wedges on a cookie sheet and sprinkle lightly with your choice of seasonings. Some people stick with pepper and a little bit of salt, but you might want to experiment with chili powder, curry powder, paprika, garlic salt, or herbs such as dill and rosemary. Just remember, a little seasoning goes a long way.

Now bake your jo-jos in the oven for about 40 minutes or until they are golden brown and crispy on the outside. Turn them once or twice while baking so that they cook evenly. Let them cool a bit, and enjoy a bite of Idaho!

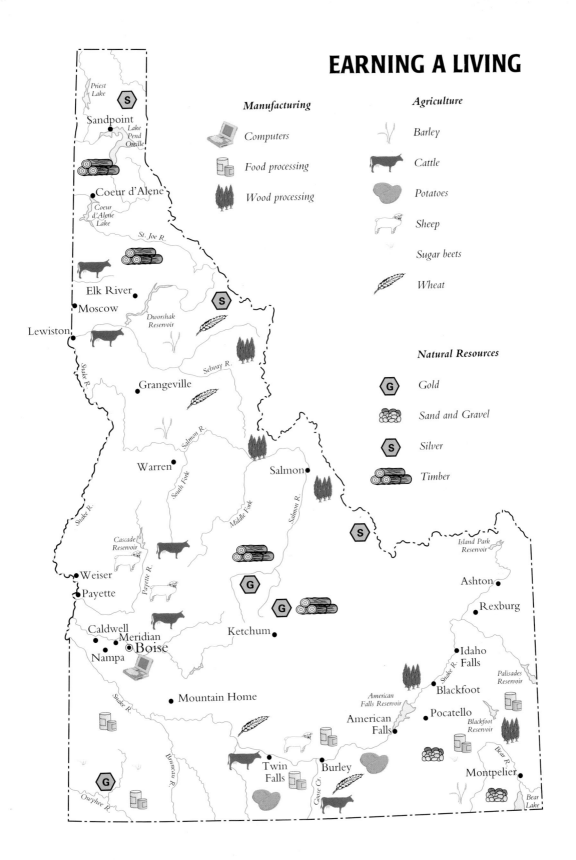

EARNING A LIVING

Manufacturing

Computers

Food processing

Wood processing

Agriculture

Barley

Cattle

Potatoes

Sheep

Sugar beets

Wheat

Natural Resources

G Gold

Sand and Gravel

S Silver

Timber

sell. Idaho is the country's top trout producer. If you order trout in a restaurant, chances are it came from an Idaho hatchery.

TIMBER AND MINING

Idaho's mining and timber industries suffered in the 1980s and early 1990s when demand for their minerals and wood products fell. Prices dropped, and many people lost their jobs. Some timber companies went out of business. Most of those that survived did so by streamlining and modernizing—in other words, by employing fewer people. Many mines also closed, leading to high unemployment in the mining districts of the north.

Today, the mining industry employs only about 3,100 Idahoans. "You hear a lot of talk about moving people into new jobs for the future," a thirty-nine-year-old Kellogg man said bitterly after losing his job. "You can't tell me someone's going to teach me to be a computer programmer, when all I've ever done is work in the mines." Some aspects of Idaho's economy may be booming, but hard times are still a reality in communities that have long depended upon a single industry.

Despite economic ups and downs, lumber production remains Idaho's fifth-ranking industry in terms of income, while mining ranks sixth. Idaho's mines produce significant amounts of lead, silver, phosphate, and other minerals. Idaho is called the Gem

For a fee, anyone can dig or pan for star garnets at the Emerald Creek Garnet Area in the Idaho Panhandle National Forests.

State, and not just because of the phony "gem of the mountains" name. Many gems have been mined in Idaho. The most commercially important is the garnet, a deep red stone. Idaho's state stone is the star garnet, a special kind of garnet more valuable than either the ruby or sapphire. There's also gold in the Idaho hills. Some is mined commercially, and some is teased out of riverbanks and hillsides by individual prospectors who have staked claims not too different from those of the long-ago gold rush.

CATCHING THE TOURIST DOLLAR

These days a different kind of gold rush is happening along Idaho's streams and in its mountains. People are coming to Idaho in ever-increasing numbers to fish, hike, camp, run white-water rapids, rock climb, ski, and mountain bike. Tourism and travel are the state's third-largest industry. The sport-fishing industry alone brings $150 million to Idaho each year in the form of money spent on gas, food, lodging, bait, tackle, guide services, boat rentals, and fishing and boating permits.

From vacationing families and retirees cruising the scenic byways in recreational vehicles to hard-core, no-frills backpackers, Idaho seems to have something for everyone. Hiker Dean Bethea reported that a three-day hike around the Seven Devils Range featured magnificent views, challenging climbs, and a brisk swim in a mountain lake. He left "tired, exhilarated, and convinced that the Northwest has few ranges that compare with the Seven Devils when it comes to scenery and the variety of trails."

What draws people to Idaho? And why do so many come back

Hikers near White Cloud Mountain. Recreation has become big business for Idaho.

again and again? Larry EchoHawk, a man of mixed white and Native American descent who has served as the state attorney general and been a candidate for governor, thinks he has the answer: "Idaho is what America once was, and what the rest of the nation now wants to be."

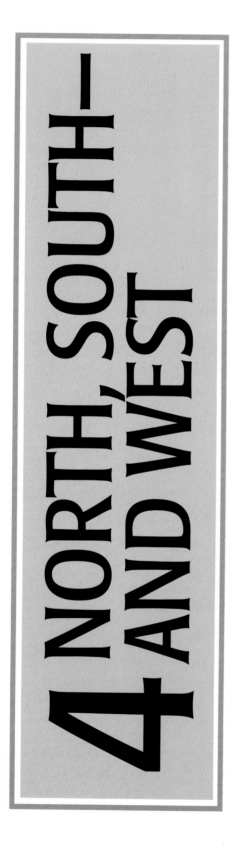

4 NORTH, SOUTH— AND WEST

People in the Gem State often talk of "two Idahos." Many times they mean north Idaho and south Idaho. Sometimes they mean city and country, Boise and its suburbs contrasted with the rural rest of the state. And sometimes they mean new Idaho and old Idaho— people who have moved to the state in recent years and those whose roots go back a generation or more.

But despite these contrasts, one thing is true everywhere in Idaho: it is part of the West. Scuffed boots and weathered pickup trucks are part of the scenery. Horseback riding and hunting are familiar parts of life for lots of people, including many teenagers.

Perhaps you'll be reminded that you're in the West as you drive up a rutted mountain road in Clearwater National Forest. Traffic signs are scarce there, but most of them are bullet-riddled, because a lot of gun-totin' Westerners seem to regard signs as targets. Or you may be driving along Interstate 84 on a windy February day, heading for the urban attractions of Boise, when suddenly a mass—no, a herd—of golden brown tumbleweeds appears on the horizon, and traffic stops while hundreds of them whirl and bound across four lanes. At times like that even someone in a business suit feels like a cowboy.

"City people drive trucks these days because they want to look like they do real work," scoffed the owner of one muddy pickup. You could see a hard-working old truck like this one on any country road in Idaho.

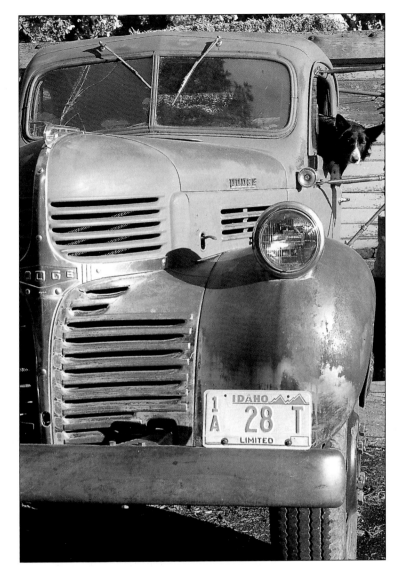

A STATE WITH THREE CAPITALS

Idahoans joke that theirs is the only state with three capitals—Boise, Spokane, and Salt Lake City. There is some truth to the joke. Idaho's panhandle is geographically the same as eastern Washington, and many people there remember that the region wanted to be part of Washington, not Idaho. When people in Coeur d'Alene or Kellogg have an errand to do in a bigger city, it's much easier for them to drive to Spokane, just across the border in Washington, than to spend hours traveling to Boise. Geography is still a powerful barrier to travel in Idaho. Several east-west routes cross the state, but only one paved road, Highway 95, runs north-south through its length, squeezed between the bulk of the central mountains and the gorge of Hells Canyon.

In the same way, many people in rural southeastern Idaho feel culturally and geographically closer to Utah, and to its nearby capital in Salt Lake City, than to Boise. Much of southeastern Idaho was settled by Mormons from Utah, and the Mormon heritage is still strong in the region.

Today Idaho has more Mormons than any state except Utah, and more of Idaho's churchgoers belong to the Church of Jesus Christ of Latter-Day Saints than to any other church. The Roman Catholic faith also has many followers, especially in the north—a legacy of the early Catholic missions. Protestant churches are also active in Idaho, including some fundamentalist groups. Although not all Idahoans are religious, many of those who are religious have strong feelings about the importance of church and the Bible in daily life.

ETHNIC IDAHO

Idaho's population may be small, but it is growing. It increased by 20 percent between 1990 and 1997, and in 1998 a major national moving company announced that Idaho ranked fourth among the states as a destination for movers. It seems that word of Idaho's attractions is getting out. A motel keeper in Twin Falls has seen signs of growth—and he's a little concerned about it. "It's only been in the last couple of years that we've had more than a million people here," he remarked in 1998. He compared life in Idaho to memories of a trip to Chicago thirty years earlier. "So

The Mormon temple in Boise

ETHNIC IDAHO

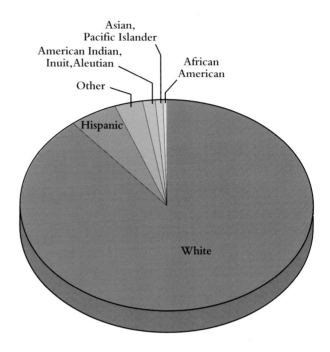

Asian, Pacific Islander

American Indian, Inuit, Aleutian

African American

Other

Hispanic

White

many people—who could live like that?" he asked, shaking his head.

"Yes, Idaho is changing, but not fast enough," declares one Boise woman who moved to Idaho three years ago to take a job she loves. "I moved here from California," she says. "The way some people here act, that's a crime in itself. There's a lot to like in Idaho, but it can be a very closed-minded place. Boise is okay, but I don't think I could ever feel at home out in the countryside."

Perhaps one reason this woman doesn't feel completely at home in Idaho is that she is Asian American. Idaho is a very white state. Fewer than 6 percent of its residents are of black, Asian, South Pacific, Hispanic, or Native American descent. Once you go beyond Boise and the other urban centers of the Snake River Plain, it's rare to see a person of color.

Today Idaho's small Indian population includes representatives of the Kutenai, Coeur d'Alene, Nez Perce, Shoshone-Bannock, and Northern Paiute tribes. Many, but not all, of the Idaho Indians live on the state's four reservations. They hold various events—such as Chief Lookingglass Days in Kamiah, a town on the Nez Perce Reservation, and the Shoshone-Bannock Indian Festival in Fort Hall—both to celebrate their heritage and to attract tourists.

The state's Hispanic population has grown in recent years. Some of the newcomers are migrant workers who came to pick crops and decided to stay. In 1994, the U.S. Census Bureau estimated that there were more than 11,000 Spanish-speaking residents in southeastern Idaho alone. Polo Yanez of Rexburg operates a radio station to serve their needs. It broadcasts in Spanish, supported by advertisements from local Hispanic-owned businesses. Yanez remembers how hard it was for him to feel good about his Hispanic identity after moving from Texas to Blackfoot, Idaho, in 1971. "I had a pretty bad time," he recalls. "I never got adjusted." Today Yanez operates his radio station partly as a business and partly as a service to his fellow Hispanic Idahoans. "It promotes self-confidence in the community," he says.

Idaho is home to several thousand people of Basque heritage. Their ancestors moved to Idaho from the mountains of northern Spain between 1890 and 1920 to work as sheepherders, miners, and construction laborers. Many sent for wives and families to join them, giving rise to a community that kept the Basque language and customs alive in and around the Boise area. Today the Basque Museum and Cultural Center in Boise honors those early settlers and serves as a focus for Idahoans of Basque descent.

A visitor from China helps celebra ethnic and cultural diversity at the Idaho International Folk Dance Festival in Rexburg.

An Indian boy pre-
pares for a traditional
dance.

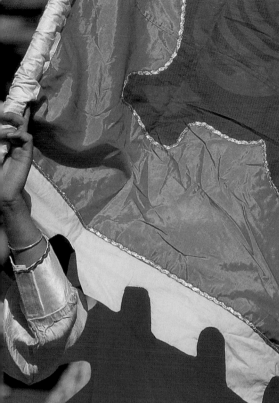

Idaho's Basques still celebrate the traditional clothing and customs of their European
homeland during festivals and other special
events.

GOING TO EXTREMES?

Many Idahoans live in small communities with very little ethnic diversity. This way of life can be comforting, but it also has a dark side. People who are not exposed to change and diversity can become intolerant and prejudiced. In recent years racist groups that promote white supremacy have established themselves in northern Idaho. But as one Lewiston woman points out, "They're

Small-town life still appeals to many Idahoans, who must balance its draw-backs with its advantages.

here, but they're not in the majority. Most of us are deeply embarrassed to have our state identified with hatred and violence."

Other offbeat groups, building on Idaho's reputation as the home of individualists, have carved out places for themselves in Idaho's conservative political environment. The state is home to some people and organizations that strongly disagree with the U.S. government on such issues as gun laws, taxes, and immigration. Some of them regard themselves as living outside U.S. law, which they claim now violates the original spirit of the Constitution. A few believe that the country, or even the world, is about to come to an end.

Most of the time these extremists have little impact on the outside world, but occasionally violence erupts into the headlines. This happened at Ruby Ridge in northern Idaho in 1992. An eleven-day standoff between federal agents and Randy Weaver, a white supremacist and critic of the government who was charged with breaking firearms laws, ended with three people dead. Although not many Idahoans agree with Weaver's ideas, many feel that the Federal Bureau of Investigation caused the bloodshed.

AN AMERICAN PARADISE

"Throughout Idaho are men who have settled in the state and natives who refuse to leave simply because the side rewards of living there are greater than the greater money they might make outside. They like small towns and small-city associations, and they like free space, and they fill their eyes with grandeur and their ears with the great silence of the mountains." A. B. Guthrie wrote these words for *Holiday* magazine in 1954. To many Idahoans they still ring true.

The people of Idaho like living in a place where neighbors know each other, and where no one passes by a stranded motorist on a winter road. They like being close to wild land and the freedom it represents—even a Boise office worker is just a short drive from pristine forests and quiet mountain paths. One accountant there keeps his snowboard in his office, ready for an after-work jaunt to the nearby hills. "Maybe I'll only take it out three or four times a year," he admits. "But it's just cool to know I *can*."

Many fairs, festivals, and events in Idaho honor the state's pioneer heritage. Coeur d'Alene Indians celebrate a pilgrimage in which they reenact the arrival of the Black Robes, the early Catholic missionaries. Lewiston hosts one of Idaho's many rodeos, and Orofino has Lumberjack Days, in which loggers from many states compete in such events as logrolling. At the Mountain Man Rendezvous, held at Massacre Rocks State Park near American Falls, people relive the days of the mountain men with knife-throwing contests and tepee villages. Every June fiddlers from around the world gather in the farming town of Weiser for the National Oldtime Fiddlers' Contest, where music fills the air and toes tap late into the night.

Other events celebrate the land and its bounty. There's a Cherry Festival at harvesttime in Emmett, an Apple Blossom Festival in Payette, and, of course, Idaho Annual Spud Day, celebrated in the potato-growing community of Shelley. Seasonal events range from summer white-water kayak "rodeos" on the Payette River to Christmastime tree lightings and reenactments of pioneer holidays.

Calf roping at the Snake River Stampede, one of the state's many rodeos

Idaho's cultural life is as rich and varied as its landscape. Boise has professional ballet, symphony, and opera companies as well as museums, theaters, and a lively art gallery scene. Cultural life is not confined to the capital, however. In many communities, events such as the Lionel Hampton Jazz Festival, the Sun Valley Summer Symphony, and the Idaho Shakespeare Festival entertain and enlighten Idahoans.

With its homespun communities, its natural beauty, and a generous helping of culture, is Idaho an American paradise? Ask the people who are flocking to buy homes in the Teton Valley in the eastern part of the state. During the 1990s, Teton County's population grew faster than that of any other Idaho county, rising by 54 percent in just seven years. Growth has not been painless, however. One farmer made headlines when, after losing a battle to block a housing development on what used to be farmland, he put up a sign warning potential buyers of the "hazards" of rural life, such as cow manure and barnyard smells.

A young musician at the National Oldtime Fiddler's Contest

On the shore of beautiful Payette Lake in west-central Idaho is the town of McCall. In summer it is a paradise of swimming, boating, fishing, and sunny outdoor fun. But what about winter? In 1924, a resident of McCall came up with a plan to banish the midwinter doldrums—dogsled races. It was the beginning of a yearly tradition. Local people began building snow sculptures, and in the 1960s a sculpture contest became an official part of the festivities.

Today the McCall Winter Carnival is one of Idaho's liveliest events. The carnival includes many different snow-sculpting competitions, ranging from children's contests to a competition that draws professional snow sculptors from around the world. A visitor to McCall during the festival should not be surprised to see a giant snow cowboy riding an even bigger sea serpent or a lumbering family of two-story-tall polar bears. "There's some absolutely incredible work," contest organizer Diane Wiegand said during the 1998 carnival. "There's a tree of life with different animals in it, a pirate, an abstract guitar player . . . I'm just glad I'm not one of the judges."

The spread of the highway network and the growth of nearby cities are causing many small Idaho railroad towns to fade quietly away.

The conflict between this farmer and the property developer is a sign of the tension between the forces that are changing Idaho and those that want to keep it unchanged. But Idaho has already changed a great deal since 1900, when 6 percent of its people lived in cities and 94 percent lived in the country. By 1990, more than 57 percent of Idaho's population was urban—a trend toward city life that will likely continue.

Cities may be growing, but some small towns are dying. Idaho's landscape is dotted with shrinking communities like King Hill in the Snake River Plain. "It was a good place to raise your children," recalls Peggy Marnock, who emigrated from Scotland in the early 1930s. "I'll bet there's not a hundred people here now. Mostly retired folks."

To some people, paradise means doing it your own way, and Idaho has plenty of room for them. In 1993, Alanna Lefsaker wrote about her family's experiences in Idaho: "Seven years were in a very remote area near Hells Canyon and we loved it, but our kids turned into teens and 60 miles from the nearest town made it a little difficult for them to make friends, so we now live 12 miles from town on 155 acres. We like it here, too. It's almost as remote since we're at the end of the road and the road is a very rough one." For many Idahoans, the rough road is the road to contentment.

5 INSPIRING IDAHOANS

Idaho may be sparsely populated, but it has produced a number of notable characters who have made their mark in the state and in the wider world. Among them are writers, politicians, businesspeople, and sports legends.

LITERARY LIFE

A number of well-known writers have been associated with Idaho. Ezra Pound, one of the foremost poets of the twentieth century, was born in Hailey, although he spent very little of his life there. Edgar Rice Burroughs, creator of Tarzan, spent a few years living and working in southern Idaho around the turn of the century, before his adventure tales made him famous. Novelist Ernest Hemingway was a frequent visitor to Sun Valley and lived in Ketchum at the end of his life. Other authors are true *Idaho* writers whose work was inspired by the state's landscape and history. For example, Vardis Fisher wrote many books about Idaho frontier life, the Lewis and Clark expedition, and the mountain men.

One of Idaho's most beloved writers was Carol Ryrie Brink, who was born in 1895 in the small town of Moscow, where she was raised by her pioneer grandmother. As a child Carol entertained herself by reading and making up her own stories. Later, while attending the University of Idaho, she wrote for the college news-

Ezra Pound's complex, worldly, modern poetry might well have baffled some of those who knew him as a child in 1880s Idaho.

Novelist Edgar Rice Burroughs set his most famous scenes of wilderness adventure in Africa, but he had more real experience of Idaho.

Carol Ryrie Brink drew upon her family's pioneer history in Moscow, Idaho, when she wrote books for children and adults.

paper. Beginning in 1933 she published nearly thirty books. Her best-known work is *Caddie Woodlawn*, a novel based on the stories her grandmother had told her about growing up on the Wisconsin frontier. In 1936, it won the Newbery Medal for best children's book of the year.

Brink wrote three children's books about life in the Moscow region—*All over Town*, *Louly*, and *Two Are Better than One*. The Moscow area also provided the setting for four novels for adult readers: *Buffalo Coat*, *Strangers in the Forest*, *Four Girls on a Homestead*, and *Snow in the River*, providing a personal view of life in pioneer Idaho.

BUFFALO COAT

Carol Ryrie Brink's novel *Buffalo Coat* paints a picture of life in the small town of Moscow, Idaho, in pioneer days. An early passage captures the haunting emptiness of the Palouse wheat fields:

At the corner where the road turned up to the cemetery, the Stevens house stood, narrow and bleak and weathered. It was built on the plan of a city house which had been forced into perpendicular lines because of close neighbors and narrow lots. It was the house a city man would build, not a farmer. Yet there were no other houses for miles—only the flat yellow of stubble or the green of young wheat merging into the rippling gold of fruition or the long white undulations of the snow. It was brutal in its loneliness. A man's mind might grow strange and secret here, if he kept away from his neighbors. He might be troubled by fantastic thoughts which would never occur to him on a high stool in a narrow office with people passing to and fro.

J.R. "Jack" Simplot built an enormous business empire on the humble spud, the root of his fortune.

BUSINESS AND POLITICS

If there's one person who made the potato an international symbol of Idaho, it is J. R. "Jack" Simplot, whose family moved from Iowa to Idaho when he was a small boy. Simplot dropped out of high school and went into business for himself as a horse trader and small-time farmer. He didn't stay small-time for long.

Simplot bought a farm and got into the potato business. "I knew how to get a penny from a potato, and when I got that penny I saved it," he once said. By 1941, Simplot was shipping more potatoes than any other farmer in Idaho and supplying huge quantities of dried potatoes to the U.S. Army. After the war Simplot's company came up with a way to produce frozen french fries, eventually becoming the major supplier of fries to the McDonald's fast-food empire. While never losing his focus on potatoes, Simplot branched

Idaho politician Frank Church (left) never made it to the White House, but wilderness lovers are grateful for what he did accomplish.

out into other areas of food processing as well as into mining and fertilizer production. Long recognized as one of the state's most important people and one of the nation's richest, Simplot has given millions of dollars to Idaho institutions such as the College of Idaho. "I never wanted to live anywhere else—I know a good place when I find it," he has said of the state he loves. "It's been good to me."

Frank Church showed his love for Idaho in a different way. Born in Boise, the grandson of an Idaho gold rush pioneer, Church grew up admiring well-known Idaho politician William E. Borah, who served in the U.S. Senate for thirty-three years. Like Borah, Church studied law and then entered politics. He was elected to the U.S. Senate in 1956, at the age of thirty-two, and remained a senator until 1981.

In 1976, Church made an announcement on the steps of the old courthouse in Idaho City. "It is never too late—nor are the odds too great—to try," he said. "In that spirit the West was won, and in that spirit I now declare my candidacy for president of the United States." Church later withdrew his candidacy in favor of fellow Democrat Jimmy Carter, who won the election.

Although he never became president, Church was a leading figure in national politics. Over the years his steadfast liberal stand on key issues put him out of step with some of Idaho's conservative voters. Church criticized American involvement in the Vietnam War and sponsored an investigation of misdeeds by government agencies such as the Central Intelligence Agency. Church was also a strong supporter of conservation and led the fight to pass the Wilderness Act of 1964. Back in Idaho irate loggers and miners, disgusted with their environmentalist senator, hanged a dummy

"CHINA POLLY" OF IDAHO

One colorful figure from Idaho's pioneer past has become a state legend. Idahoans remember her for her dramatic origins and generous hospitality during Idaho's early days.

Lalu Nathoy was born in China in 1853. To raise money to feed the family, her parents sold her into slavery. The events of her early life would have destroyed many people, but Lalu Nathoy was a survivor. Eventually she wound up in a saloon in Warrens, Idaho. The locals called her "China Polly" and, despite anti-Chinese prejudice, many of them came to like and respect her.

When a well-liked local man named Charlie Bemis was shot in a brawl, Polly nursed him back to health. Upon his recovery Charlie married Polly. The story went around that Charlie had won Polly in a poker game, but that was nothing more than frontier myth-making.

The Bemises left Warrens for a homestead in the Salmon River canyon. Living off the land was hard, but they enjoyed many happy years on their farm. Polly, who often cared for sick and injured neighbors, was very popular. "Every time a wandering prospector came to the Bemis farm he was not only sure of a hospitable welcome . . . but he was also sure to be loaded down with pies and cakes to be delivered to Polly's old friends," says one account of her life. A cherished member of the community, Polly became something of a local landmark—the slave girl who had become a homesteader. Today Polly and Charlie Bemis are buried side by side on their old homestead.

bearing Church's name. A more lasting monument, however, is the Frank Church River of No Return Wilderness in central Idaho, one of the largest protected wilderness areas in the nation.

Picabo Street's skiing career has included both dramatic victories and devastating injuries. "No half measures—I go out there to win," she says.

A MODERN SPORTS HERO

No one is a better symbol of hip, young, sports-oriented Idaho than skier Picabo (pronounced peekaboo) Street. Born in 1971 in tiny Triumph, Idaho, population thirteen, Street grew up in an old mining shack and learned to ski at an early age by chasing her father and brother down the slopes at the resorts of nearby Sun Valley. In the mid-1980s, Street began climbing through the ranks of America's female skiers. She won several championships before suffering a knee injury in 1989.

After training to rebuild strength in her knee, Street returned to racing, winning a reputation for her flashy style and zany antics as much as for her outstanding performance on the slopes. In the 1994–1995 season she won six international meets, became the first American to win the World Cup skiing title, and brought home a silver medal from the winter Olympics. In 1998, overcoming several recent injuries, she won a gold medal at the Winter Olympics in Nagano, Japan. Fans all over the United States—but especially those in ski lodges and small-town bars across Idaho—whooped with joy. "This is the Olympics, baby," Street had written in a newspaper column just before the event. "I'm going to be fast or I'm going to go out." Sadly, Street suffered a serious knee injury in another event later in the Olympics. Although the future of her skiing career was in doubt, she had proven to everyone that she was a champion.

6 GEM STATE ROAD TRIP

Idaho has many treasures that can be discovered on a road trip from north to south. "Watch out," one resident warned a visitor. "You might like it so much you'll never get out."

NORTHERN IDAHO

The Idaho Panhandle has the West's largest concentration of lakes. It's a wonderland for kayakers and canoeists. Golfers face an unusual challenge at the Coeur d'Alene Resort's course. Part of the course is located on an island in Lake Coeur d'Alene, and players must ride a boat out to play it.

East of the lake is the Silver Valley, the scene of much mining history. The entire town of Wallace, called the Silver Capital of the World, has been registered as a National Historic Place. At the Sierra Silver Mine, you can hop aboard a trolley that will take you for a seventy-five-minute tour through the tunnels, where you'll see mining equipment in operation, discover what silver ore looks like (it's not always silver), and learn how miners get the earth to give up its treasures.

Farther south is Lewiston. As you gaze across the Snake River at the rolling wheat fields of Washington State stretching away as far as the eye can see, you may not realize that Lewiston is a Pacific Ocean port. Thanks to channel dredging and locks around the

Idaho's Palouse country, home of the Appaloosa horse and an important wheat-farming region

many dams, oceangoing vessels can travel 470 miles from the mouth of the Columbia River to Lewiston to take on cargoes of grain, timber, and potatoes. While you're in the area, visit the Nez Perce National Historical Park and Museum, which has a fine collection of Nez Perce artifacts. Not far away is Spalding, named for Idaho's early missionary. The Saint Joseph's Mission, built in 1874, still stands nearby.

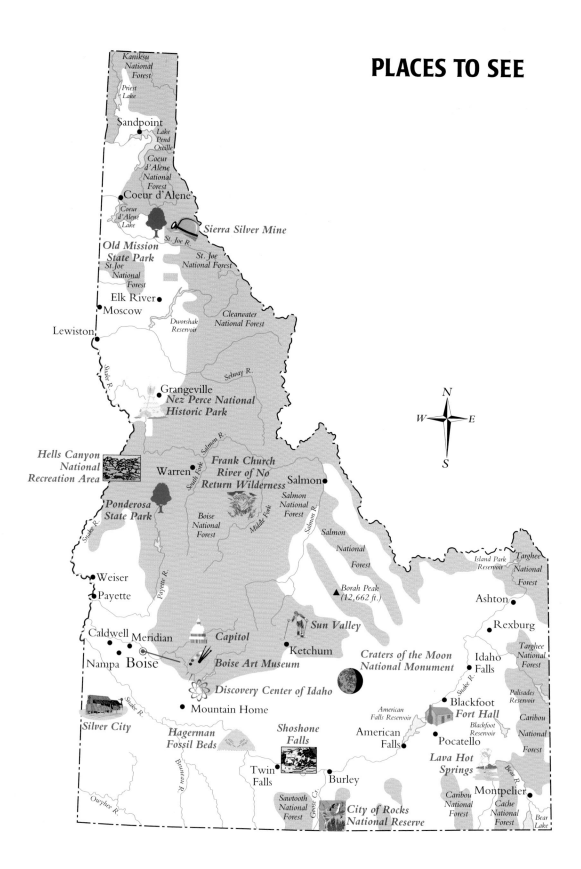

PLACES TO SEE

Kaniksu National Forest

Priest Lake

Sandpoint

Lake Pend Oreille

Coeur d'Alene National Forest

Coeur d'Alene

Coeur d'Alene Lake

Sierra Silver Mine

St. Joe R.

Old Mission State Park

St. Joe National Forest

St. Joe National Forest

Elk River

Moscow

Lewiston

Dworshak Reservoir

Clearwater National Forest

Snake R.

Selway R.

Grangeville

Nez Perce National Historic Park

Salmon R.

Hells Canyon National Recreation Area

Warren

South Fork

Frank Church River of No Return Wilderness

Salmon

Salmon National Forest

Ponderosa State Park

Boise National Forest

Middle Fork

Salmon R.

Salmon National Forest

Island Park Reservoir

Targhee National Forest

Weiser

Payette R.

Payette

▲ *Borah Peak (12,662 ft.)*

Ashton

Rexburg

Snake R.

Caldwell   Meridian

Capitol

Sun Valley

Ketchum

Craters of the Moon National Monument

Idaho Falls

Targhee National Forest

Nampa   Boise

Boise Art Museum

Discovery Center of Idaho

Palisades Reservoir

Mountain Home

Snake R.

American Falls Reservoir

Blackfoot

Fort Hall

Blackfoot Reservoir

Caribou National Forest

Silver City

Hagerman Fossil Beds

Shoshone Falls

American Falls

Pocatello

Lava Hot Springs

Bruneau R.

Twin Falls

Burley

Caribou National Forest

Montpelier

Bear R.

Cache National Forest

Ouyhee R.

Sawtooth National Forest

Goose Cr.

City of Rocks National Reserve

Bear Lake

N W E S

CENTRAL IDAHO

Lewiston and the town of Riggins to the south are gateways to the extraordinary world of Hells Canyon. At its deepest point the canyon measures 8,000 feet from mountain peak to surging water—deeper than the Grand Canyon. Although there are gravel roads into the Hells Canyon National Recreation Area, the best way to see the canyon is by hiking along the rim or from a boat on the river. Outfitters offer paddle- and powerboat trips through the canyon.

White water ahead! The Middle Fork of the Salmon River is one of the country's most challenging sites for rafting and kayaking.

The glory of north-central Idaho is the great River of No Return. If you can arrange a white-water trip on the Salmon River, you'll float or paddle past Indian petroglyphs (carvings on cliff walls), abandoned mine workings, and isolated ranches and homesteads tucked into folds in the hills. You may also experience a cold dunking when your boat flips over in a rapid, so be sure to wear a life preserver!

Except for the roads that snake through the Clearwater Valley in the west, central Idaho is largely roadless. An exception is Highway 12, which roughly follows the route of Lewis and Clark across Idaho. A drive along this highway will introduce you to the Lochsa River, which has been designated a National Wild and Scenic River, and to a magnificent stretch of national forest, dotted with hot springs and trailheads. At the eastern border of Idaho it crosses Lolo Pass where Lewis and Clark did.

If your vehicle is sturdy, you may try venturing onto some of the twisting, rutted forest roads that wind into valleys and along ridges. Soon, however, those roads peter out and there's nothing but roadless wilderness in front of you. Some wilderness explorers claim that Idaho offers some of the finest hiking in the world. "Backpacking in the Bitterroots is the experience of a lifetime," claims Brenda Charris of Oregon. "It was like being alone in a perfect world before people arrived on the scene."

SOUTHERN IDAHO

Southern Idaho has the largest share of the state's city lights. In Boise, the capitol building is not to be missed. This lovely domed

Autumn turns the hills around Boise to gold, a shining backdrop to a lively, fast-growing city. The dome marks the state capitol.

structure is patterned after the U.S. Capitol in Washington, D.C., but has some distinctively Idahoan touches. For example, Idaho's capitol is heated by water from a geothermal well, an energy source increasingly popular in a state filled with hot springs and steam vents. And the impressive statue of George Washington on horseback is not made of marble or bronze. It was carved from a massive yellow pine by an Austrian immigrant named Charles Ostner, who had only a picture of Washington on a postage stamp to serve as a model.

A good way to see Boise's historic and downtown neighborhoods is from the tour train, which provides a one-hour narrated ride through the city. But if you'd rather explore on your own, Boise is a comfortable walking city, with coffee shops on many corners, café tables on sidewalks during mild weather, and plenty of shade trees. In fact, the city's name means "wooded" in French. It was given

Hop aboard the tour train for an informative look at downtown Boise.

by French-Canadian trappers who were grateful for the shade trees along the Boise River in the otherwise sunbaked landscape of the Snake River Plain.

Relics of Idaho's history dot the southwestern part of the state. Silver City in the Owyhee Mountains is the "Queen of Idaho Ghost Towns," a community that formed after miners struck gold and silver nearby in the 1860s and then faded away after the 1920s. A few people still live in Silver City, but the old drugstore and schoolhouse are now museums. Silver City is well worth a trip, but only in good weather—the twenty-three-mile dirt road can be treacherous. Easier to reach is Idaho City, north of Boise. For a time during the gold rush of the 1860s, it was the biggest community in Idaho. Boardwalks and buildings from that era survive. Many of the colorful structures now house modern businesses.

Southern Idaho has many unusual geological and geographic features. The Bruneau Dunes are a cluster of sand dunes that rise nearly five hundred feet above the plain. Fossils of many creatures that once roamed this part of North America, including ancient horses, mastodons, and saber-toothed cats, have been found at Hagerman Fossil Beds. Just outside the town of Twin Falls is Shoshone Falls, a waterfall higher than New York's famed Niagara Falls. In spring, when the Snake River is at its highest, torrents of foam plunge 212 feet to a turbulent pool below. To the southeast, near Oakley, is the City of Rocks National Reserve. Early pioneers who wandered into this area were awestruck. Out of the rolling sagebrush landscape loom sixty-story granite columns, looking like ghostly, silent skyscrapers.

North of Twin Falls lies Sun Valley, where you may spot movie

*For a few exciting years in the 1860s, the mining camp called Idaho City had
two hundred businesses and was the largest city in the Pacific Northwest.*

IDAHO'S MOONSCAPE

One early visitor called it "a desolate and awful waste." Another wrote that it was "the strangest 75 square miles on the North American continent." They were describing a place in southeastern Idaho where the land's volcanic past is visible on its tortured surface— an area covered with the black, crumbling remains of past lava flows.

The Shoshone never lived in this region, although they traveled over it. Pioneers gave it a wide berth—not only was water hard to find in the sunbaked black lava wastes, but the sharp rock would cut their animals' feet to ribbons. Settlers and ranchers considered the lava wasteland worthless. In 1924, however, the U.S. Congress recognized its geological interest and named it Craters of the Moon National Monument. Today it is one of the state's major tourist attractions. Drivers and bicyclists can follow a seven-mile loop past lava tubes, cones, caves, and other dramatic features.

At first glance the huge expanse of twisted, ribbed lava may seem as barren as the lunar surface for which it is named. But look more closely. A swift, striped ground squirrel is scooting between two rocks. Overhead a prairie falcon soars lazily, and nearer at hand a songbird pipes from a sunny ledge. In spring Craters of the Moon blooms with short-lived but dazzling wildflowers. A different kind of life blooms there in midwinter, when brightly clad cross-country skiers glide along snow-covered trails through the lava wilderness.

"They look just like those pyramids in Egypt!" exclaimed one ten-year-old visitor to the Bruneau Dunes.

stars sharing the slopes with tanned teenage snowboarders. Sun Valley, along with the nearby towns of Hailey and Ketchum, is Idaho's center of glittering celebrity life, but the surrounding area is home to ordinary, hardworking folks as well.

Eastern Idaho offers vistas of the magnificent spires of the Grand Tetons. One Twin Falls resident recalled showing a photograph of the Tetons to someone back east years ago. "That's a painting," the New Yorker scoffed. "There aren't really any mountains that are pointed like that."

Southeastern Idaho may not have sky-piercing crags or mile-deep canyons, but it has gentle charms of its own, with many scenic byways cutting through green hills. Bear Lake is a tranquil fishing and boating spot. Lava Hot Springs, with pools heated by the

Sun Valley was the first European-style ski resort to open in the United States. "And the skiing's still great," says an Oregon woman who visits the resort every winter.

earth's volcanic forces, was once a camp shared by Shoshone and Bannock Indians. Today it has a resort with an Olympic-sized pool, tennis courts, and a golf course.

As you explore southeastern Idaho you'll also find Soda Springs, where hot mineral water gushes forth from thirty springs. Pioneers called one of them Beer Springs. Its water doesn't taste much like

Mountains are never far away in Idaho. Flat farmland in the east ends abruptly at the Teton Mountains, one of the most scenic ranges in the Rockies.

beer—but the pioneers had been on the trail for a long, thirsty time. The Oregon Trail ran through Soda Springs, and foot-deep wagon ruts can still be seen on the local golf course. End your tour of Idaho where the pioneers used to begin it. Wrote one of them as his wagon train approached Soda Springs: "Here we enter the Snake countrie."

THE FLAG: The flag shows the state seal against a blue background. Below the seal is a scroll that reads "State of Idaho." Idaho's flag was first adopted in 1907 and readopted in 1957.

THE SEAL: The woman holding scales in Idaho's state seal symbolizes liberty, justice, and equality. The miner represents the state's mineral wealth, the elk's head stands for its wildlife, the pine tree for its forests, and the grain for its agriculture. The seal was originally adopted in 1891 and was readopted in 1957.

STATE SURVEY

Statehood: July 3, 1890

Origin of Name: A miner made up the name *Idaho*. He claimed it was an
Indian word that meant "gem of the mountains."

Nickname: Gem State

Capital: Boise

Motto: Let It Be Perpetual

Bird: Mountain bluebird

Flower: Syringa

Tree: Western white pine

Gem: Star garnet

Horse: Appaloosa

Syringa

Appaloosa

HERE WE HAVE IDAHO

The music for the Idaho state song was composed in 1915 under the title "Garden of Paradise." In 1917, McKinley Helm, a student at the University of Idaho, wrote lyrics to it, and it was adopted as the university's song. In 1931, with a revised set of lyrics, the song was recognized as the official state song. It is also known as "Our Idaho."

Words by
Bethel Packenham and McKinley Helm

Music by
Sallie Hume-Douglas

Folk Dance: Square dance

Fish: Cutthroat trout

Fossil: Hagerman horse fossil

GEOGRAPHY

Highest Point: 12,662 feet above sea level, at Mount Borah

Lowest Point: 710 feet, in Lewiston

Area: 83,574 square miles

Greatest Distance, North to South: 483 miles

Greatest Distance, East to West: 316 miles

Bordering States: Oregon and Washington to the west, Montana and Wyoming to the east, Nevada and Utah to the south

Hottest Recorded Temperature: 118°F in Orofino on July 28, 1934

Coldest Recorded Temperature: -60°F at Island Park Dam on January 18, 1943

Average Annual Precipitation: 19 inches

Major Rivers: Big Wood, Blackfoot, Boise, Bruneau, Clearwater, Payette, Pend Oreille, St. Joe, Salmon, Snake, Spokane, Weiser

Major Lakes: Alturas, Bear, Coeur d'Alene, Grays, Hayden, Henrys, Payette, Pend Oreille, Pettit, Priest, Redfish, Stanley

Trees: birch, cottonwood, Douglas fir, Engelmann spruce, hemlock, lodgepole pine, ponderosa pine, quaking aspen, western larch, western red cedar, white fir

Wild Plants: buttercup, columbine, elderberry, fireweed, huckleberry, larkspur, ocean spray, purple heather, thimbleberry, violet

Animals: beaver, black bear, bobcat, cougar, coyote, elk, mink, moose, mountain goat, otter, porcupine, prairie dog, pronghorn, raccoon, Rocky Mountain sheep, white-tailed deer

Cougar

Birds: duck, eagle, falcon, goose, hawk, heron, meadowlark, partridge, pheasant, sandhill crane

Fish: bass, catfish, crappie, cutthroat trout, kamloops trout, perch, salmon, steelhead trout, sturgeon

Endangered Animals: American peregrine falcon, bald eagle, Banbury Springs limpet, Bliss Rapids snail, Bruneau Hot springsnail, bull trout, gray wolf, grizzly bear, Idaho springsnail, Snake River physa snail, Utah valvata snail, white sturgeon, whooping crane, woodland caribou

Endangered Plants: MacFarlane's four-o'clock, Ute ladies'-tresses, water howellia

Woodland caribou

TIMELINE

Idaho History

1700s Shoshone, Nez Perce, Bannock, Paiute, Coeur d'Alene, Kutenai, and Kalispell Indians live in present-day Idaho

1803 The U.S. acquires the Louisiana Purchase, which includes Idaho

1805 Lewis and Clark cross Idaho

1809 David Thompson builds a trading post near Lake Pend Oreille, which is the first non-Indian structure in Idaho

1832 The largest trapper rendezvous ever is held at Pierre's Hole

1836 Henry and Eliza Spalding establish the region's first mission near present-day Lewiston

1842 The first pioneers on the Oregon Trail pass through Idaho

1850 Construction is completed on the Cataldo mission, the oldest standing structure in Idaho

1855 The first Mormons arrive in Idaho

1860 Franklin, Idaho's first permanent white settlement, is founded; gold is discovered on Orofino Creek

1862 The *Golden Age*, Idaho's first newspaper, begins publication in Lewiston

1863 Idaho Territory is created; U.S. troops kill 368 Shoshones at the Battle of Bear River, the worst slaughter of Indians in U.S. history

1874 Branches of the Union Pacific and Northern Pacific Railroads enter Idaho

1877 U.S. troops defeat the Nez Perce Indians

1884 One of the world's richest silver deposits is discovered in the Coeur d'Alene Mountains

1889 The University of Idaho is founded in Moscow

1890 Idaho becomes the 43rd state

1892 Violent labor struggles erupt in the mining region near Coeur d'Alene

1899 Governor Frank Steunenberg calls in federal troops to break a mining strike

1905 Former governor Frank Steunenberg is murdered

1910 Forest fires in northern Idaho rage across 3 million acres

1914 Idahoans elect Moses Alexander the nation's first Jewish governor

1938 Sun Valley, America's first ski resort, opens

1942 Japanese Americans from the West Coast are sent to Camp Minidoka, near Twin Falls, for the duration of World War II

1951 Electricity is generated from nuclear energy for the first time at a testing station near Idaho Falls

1955 Arco becomes the world's first city to receive all of its power from nuclear energy

1972 Ninety-one miners die in a fire at the Sunshine silver mine near Wardner

1975 Work is completed on the Columbia-Snake River Inland Waterway, making Lewiston the West's farthest-inland seaport

1988 Idaho voters approve a state lottery

ECONOMY

Agricultural Products: barley, beef cattle, dairy products, hay, hops, lentils, mint, onions, peas, plums, potatoes, sheep, sugar beets, wheat

Manufactured Products: chemicals, computers, electrical equipment, food products, lumber and wood products, metal products

Lumber

Natural Resources: clay, copper, garnet, gold, lead, phosphate, sand and gravel, silver, timber

Business and Trade: finance, real estate, shipping, tourism, wholesale and retail trade

CALENDAR OF CELEBRATIONS

McCall Winter Carnival McCall warms up during the dead of winter in January with a carnival that features ice sculptures, snowmobile races, parades, sleigh rides, and sled-dog contests.

Lionel Hampton Jazz Festival Each February, this prestigious event in Moscow features both performances and workshops by fifty world-renowned jazz musicians. Past performers have included Wynton Marsalis, Ella Fitzgerald, and of course, Lionel Hampton.

Dodge National Circuit Finals Rodeo Watch the dirt fly in Pocatello in

March when the best cowboys and cowgirls from around the country compete in such events as bronco busting and calf roping at one of the nation's largest rodeos.

Race to Robie Creek Each April thousands of people push themselves to the limit at one of the nation's most grueling races, a thirteen-mile run up and over Aldalpe Summit in Boise.

Western Days Twin Falls celebrates its rough-and-tumble past at this May event that includes a staged shootout, a chili cook-off, a barbecue, dances, and a parade.

Mountain Man Rendezvous The rugged life of the mountain men is honored in American Falls in early June. Tepees, traders, and old-fashioned weapons are all part of this rendezvous, where participants try to re-create the mountain men's life as accurately as possible.

National Oldtime Fiddlers' Contest It's impossible to sit still when the best fiddlers from around the country converge on Weiser each June. This weeklong celebration features hundreds of fiddlers competing in contests and playing at jam sessions and dances. Apart from all the music, the event also includes parades, a golf tournament, and a barbecue.

Teton Valley Hot Air Balloon Festival Few events are as breathtakingly beautiful as this July festival in Driggs, where brightly colored hot-air balloons race against a backdrop of the stunning spires of the Grand Teton Mountains. Balloon and glider rides, parades, and rodeos are all part of the fun.

Festival of San Inazio Boise's Basque community celebrates their heritage at this July event that features traditional food, dancing, and contests of strength.

Snake River Stampede One of the West's largest horse parades and a lavish breakfast kick off this July rodeo in Nampa.

Payette Whitewater Roundup Champion kayakers from all over the world come to Banks each July to compete in the world's soggiest "rodeo." These white-water experts race, surf, and perform tricks on the Payette River rapids.

Idaho International Folk Dance Festival Dancers from as far away as India, Malaysia, and Russia descend on Rexburg in late July and early August for this event. In addition to watching magnificent dancing, you can also enjoy a rodeo and country music, which give international visitors a taste of American folk culture.

Shoshone-Bannock Indian Festival and Rodeo Fort Hall hosts one of the biggest powwows in the West each August. Indians and non-Indians alike enjoy the dancing, drumming, arts and crafts, a rodeo, and even a softball tournament.

Three Islands Crossing Reenactment The drama and danger of traveling the Oregon Trail is re-created each August in Glenns Ferry. Oxen, wagons, and people dressed as pioneers splash, swim, and struggle across the Snake River at a spot where many pioneers crossed it.

Three Islands Crossing Reenactment

Idaho Spud Day Shelly celebrates Idaho's "famous potatoes" in September when thousands of Idahoans gather to compete in potato picking and peeling competitions. During the festival, you can watch a big parade while enjoying your spuds baked, fried, mashed, or scalloped.

Art in the Park Hundreds of artists display their work at this three-day event in Boise each September which attracts 150,000 visitors.

Sun Valley Swing 'n' Dixie Jazz Jamboree Each October in Sun Valley, two dozen swing, ragtime, and traditional jazz bands provide the music for five great days of dancing and fun.

Cottages and Cranberries Festival Get into the holiday spirit early at this November event in Pocatello's quaint old town. You can enjoy horse-drawn carriage rides, listen to carolers, and admire elaborate gingerbread houses and old-fashioned crafts.

STATE STARS

Joe Albertson (1906–1993) founded the Albertson's chain of grocery stores. When Albertson opened his first store in Boise in 1939, he made it larger than other groceries and included a butcher, a bakery, and an ice cream parlor, creating the first supermarket. Today, Albertson's is one of the nation's largest grocery chains. Albertson grew up in Caldwell.

Gutzon Borglum (1867–1941) was the artist who carved Mount Rushmore. Borglum, who was born in Bear Lake, was already noted for his enormous sculptures of animals and frontier life when he began work on Mount Rushmore in 1927. He continued his work sculpting the faces

Gutzon Borglum

of George Washington, Abraham Lincoln, Thomas Jefferson, and Theodore Roosevelt into the side of a mountain in South Dakota until his death.

Carol Ryrie Brink (1895–1981) wrote books for both adults and children. In 1936, she won the Newbery Medal, honoring the year's best children's novel, for *Caddie Woodlawn*, which was based on stories she had heard from her pioneer grandmother. Her novels, many of which were set near Moscow, where she was born, have a strong sense of place and a lively spirit of adventure.

Edgar Rice Burroughs (1875–1950) created the character Tarzan, a man who was raised by apes in Africa. Burroughs began writing Tarzan adventures in 1912. He eventually wrote 26 Tarzan books, and the character was featured in many movies and television programs. Burroughs grew up in Chicago but spent many summers in Idaho, where his brothers had a ranch. Later, Burroughs himself lived on and off in Idaho.

Frank Church (1924–1984), of Boise, was a U.S. Senator for 24 years. In 1956, at age 32, he was elected the youngest member of the U.S. Senate. He is perhaps best remembered for his efforts to conserve wilderness areas in Idaho. The Frank Church River of No Return Wilderness Area is named in his honor.

Philo Farnsworth (1906–1971) was an inventer known as the Father of Television. He put together the first television system, which he demonstrated in 1927. Farnsworth also made other inventions, such as the first simple electron microscope. He was born in Utah and grew up in Rigby, Idaho.

Philo Farnsworth

Vardis Fisher (1895–1968), a native of Annis, wrote novels that described the rough life on the American frontier. Some of his best-known works include *Mountain Man* and *The Children of God*.

Emma Edwards Green (1856–1942) was the artist who designed Idaho's state seal. Green, who grew up in California, went to art school in New York. Passing through Boise on her way home, she fell in love with the city and decided to stay. She soon entered a competition to design the seal of the new state and was the unanimous winner, becoming the only woman to design a state seal. She lived in Boise the rest of her life.

Ernest Hemingway (1899–1961) was one of the most influential writers of the 20th century. His direct, stripped-down prose was copied by seemingly every young writer of his time. Among his best-known books are *The Sun Also Rises* and *The Old Man and the Sea*. In 1954, he won the Nobel Prize for literature, the world's most prestigious writing award. Hemingway, who was born in Illinois, was a frequent visitor to Sun Valley before finally settling in Ketchum for the last years of his life.

Ernest Hemingway

Chief Joseph (1840–1904) was a Nez Perce chief who led 800 people, mostly women, children, and old men, on an amazing retreat through Idaho and Montana in 1877. U.S. troops had been trying to force Joseph's people onto a reservation in Idaho from their homeland in northeastern Oregon. To avoid this, he led his people on a 1,000-mile trek through the wilderness, winning many battles in Idaho along the way. U.S. troops eventually caught up with Chief Joseph in Montana near the Canadian border.

Harmon Killebrew (1936–   ), one of baseball's greatest home run hitters, was born in Payette. Playing for the Washington Senators and Minneapolis Twins, he became famous for his incredible power, which sometimes sent balls all the way out of the stadium. Killebrew is fifth in lifetime home runs in the major leagues with 573. He was elected to the National Baseball Hall of Fame in 1984.

Harmon Killebrew

Jerry Kramer (1936–   ) was a leading football player of the 1960s. He began his pro career as a guard for the Green Bay Packers in 1958 and later also became their placekicker. By the time he retired in 1968, he had been named all-pro five times and had played on five championship teams. Kramer was born in Montana and grew up in Sandpoint, Idaho.

Dan O'Brien (1966–   ) holds the world record in the decathlon, a grueling two-day track and field contest in which athletes compete in ten

Dan O'Brien

different events. He won the gold medal in the decathlon at the 1996 summer Olympics. O'Brien lives in Moscow.

Ezra Pound (1885–1972), one of the most influential poets of the 20th century, was born in Hailey. Pound believed that poetry should play an important role in society. He spent much of his life writing a long series of poems called *Cantos*, which dealt with such weighty issues as history and economics. Pound also edited several important literary journals and promoted the work of avant-garde writers.

Sacagawea (1784–1812?) was an interpreter on the Lewis and Clark expedition across the western United States. She was born in central Idaho into the Lemhi band of Shoshone. Sacagawea began traveling with Lewis and Clark in North Dakota and helped guide them peacefully through Shoshone territory. She was the only woman on the expedition and along the way gave birth to the expedition's only child.

J. R. "Jack" Simplot (1909–   ) turned a small potato farm into an empire and became one of the richest people in the country. By 1941, he was producing more potatoes than any other farmer in Idaho. He made his first million selling dried potatoes to the military. Today, his company supplies more than half of McDonald's french fries. His business is also involved in mining, frozen fruits and vegetables, and even computer parts.

Henry Spalding

Henry Spalding (1804–1874), a missionary, was the first permanent white settler in Idaho. In 1836, he and his wife, Eliza, founded the Lapwai Mission near present-day Lewiston. It included Idaho's first church, school, and sawmill.

Picabo Street (1971–   ), a champion skier, grew up in Triumph. After becoming a national junior skiing champion as a teenager, in 1995 she became the first American to win the World Cup skiing title. She has also won two Olympic medals, including a gold in the Super-G event in the 1998 Olympics. Street's fearlessness and exuberant, playful personality are as famous as her skiing prowess.

David Thompson (1770–1857) was a Canadian explorer and fur trader. In 1809, while working for the North West Company, he constructed the first non-Indian structure in Idaho, a trading post on the shores of Lake Pend Oreille. He is also famous for being the first person to travel the entire length of the Columbia River and for making an important early map of northwestern North America.

Lana Turner (1920–1995) was a popular movie star of the 1940s and 1950s, known for her elegance and poise. Turner got her start in the movies as a teenager after she was discovered at a soda fountain in Los Angeles. She became famous for her performances in such melodramas as *The Postman Always Rings Twice* and *Imitation of Life*. Turner was born in Wallace.

Lana Turner

TOUR THE STATE

Frank Church River of No Return Wilderness (Salmon) The nation's largest wilderness area outside of Alaska, this vast mountainous region covers an area larger than Rhode Island. It offers endless opportunities for hiking, white-water rafting, and wildlife watching. The wilderness also includes many soothing hot springs.

Hells Canyon National Recreation Area (Riggins) The best way to experience Hells Canyon, the deepest river canyon in North America, is either by hiking along its rim or rafting on the Snake River, more than a mile below. The canyon offers a variety of sights, ranging from cacti to Indian rock drawings to bald eagles.

Nez Perce National Historical Park (Spalding) This park includes 38 different sites from Nez Perce history, 29 of which are in Idaho. The park headquarters is the site of Lapwai Mission. Elsewhere the park preserves archaeological sites, battle sites, and geographic features important in Nez Perce mythology.

Shoshone Falls (Twin Falls) More than 200 feet tall and 1,000 feet wide, this horseshoe-shaped falls is most awe-inspiring in spring, when it is swollen with melted snow.

Fort Hall (Pocatello) The reconstruction of one of the most important trading posts on the Oregon Trail brings history to life. In addition to active blacksmith and carpentry shops, there are exhibits about Native Americans, the Oregon Trail, and the fort's history.

Sun Valley The oldest and one of the most lavish ski resorts in the country offers great alpine skiing, fast lifts, and luxurious lodgings.

City of Rocks National Reserve (Almo) Huge spires of eroded granite lure rock climbers from all over the world to this remote site. Nearby is Register Rock, where passing pioneers wrote their names.

Silver City Hidden high in the Owyhee Mountains is Idaho's best-preserved ghost town. Walking the streets of Silver City gives you the feel of what life was like in the mad days of the late 19th-century silver boom.

Harriman State Park (Island Park) Henry's Fork River, which runs through the park, is one of the country's best fly-fishing spots. The park is also ideal for hiking, biking, horseback riding, cross-country skiing, and viewing trumpeter swans, sandhill cranes, elk, beavers, and other wildlife.

Lava Hot Springs (Lava Hot Springs) In a beautiful hollow overlooking the Portneuf River, these hot springs feed several pools that stay a soothing 102 degrees.

Ponderosa State Park (McCall) Magnificent 400-year-old, 150-feet-tall Ponderosa pines tower over this park. Hiking, biking, and swimming are popular activities. There's even a lighted trail for nighttime cross-country skiing.

Hagerman Fossil Beds National Monument (Hagerman) Fossils of 140 species have been found here, making it one of the world's principal fossil beds. More than 125 full skeletons of an ancient animal called the Hagerman horse, which is the state fossil, have been uncovered at the beds.

Discovery Center of Idaho (Boise) A skeleton riding a bicycle is just one of the exhibits that makes science fun at this hands-on museum.

World Center for Birds of Prey (Boise) The center is dedicated to breeding endangered birds of prey such as peregrine falcons and releasing them into the wild. Visitors can watch presentations about birds of prey and get close-up views of injured birds.

Boise Art Museum (Boise) The pride of this beautiful museum is its collection of realist paintings, some so detailed they almost look like photographs. At night, the museum often hosts jazz concerts and other events.

Idaho Historical Museum (Boise) You'll learn about the dramatic history of Idaho's Indians, fur traders, prospectors, and pioneers at this fascinating museum. Outside are some of Boise's earliest buildings.

Basque Museum and Cultural Center (Boise) Exhibits at the museum cover Basque history, both in Idaho and in the Basque homeland on the border between France and Spain. Displays include Basque crafts and musical instruments.

Idaho's World Potato Exposition (Blackfoot) This shrine to the pride of Idaho is filled with interesting potato facts and memorabilia, including the world's largest potato chip.

Paris Stake Tabernacle (Paris) This majestic Mormon temple, made of red sandstone, was built in the 1880s.

Craters of the Moon National Monument (Arco) The twisted, contorted remains of lava flows from thousands of years ago make Craters of the Moon an eerie but fascinating place to explore.

Old Mission State Park (Cataldo) Construction was completed on the elegant Cataldo mission, the oldest standing structure in Idaho, in 1850.

Old Mission State Park

The park also features exhibits on the history of the mission and the Coeur d'Alene Indians, as well as interpretive trails.

Sierra Silver Mine (Wallace) Venturing into the depths of an old silver mine, you'll learn about the history and process of extracting the precious metal from the ground.

FUN FACTS

The world's first alpine ski lift was built in 1938 in the new ski resort of Sun Valley. It cost 25¢ per ride.

Idaho's Big Wood River has a very strange claim to fame: one section of it is four feet wide and one hundred feet deep, while a nearby section spreads to one hundred feet wide and four feet deep.

The town of Village Park has the nation's longest Main Street. It stretches for 33 miles, passing by the string of resorts that make up most of the town.

FIND OUT MORE

To learn more about Idaho, look in your local library, bookstore, or video store for these titles:

BOOKS

General State Books

Fradin, Dennis. *Idaho.* Chicago: Children's Press, 1995.

Jensen, Dwight William. *Discovering Idaho: A History.* Caldwell, ID: Caxton Printers, 1977.

Pelta, Kathy. *Idaho.* Minneapolis: Lerner Publications, 1995.

Thompson, Kathleen. *Idaho.* Milwaukee: Raintree Publishers, 1996.

Young, Virgil. *The Story of Idaho.* Moscow, ID: University of Idaho Press, 1990.

Books of Special Interest

Beck, Richard J. *100 Famous Idahoans.* Moscow, ID: Richard J. Beck, 1989.

Carter, Alden. *The Shoshoni.* New York: Franklin Watts, 1989.

Churchwell, Mary Jo. *The Cabin on Sawmill Creek.* Caldwell, ID: Caxton Printers, 1997.

Just, Rick. *Idaho Snapshots*. Boise: Tamarack Books, 1990.

Morgan, Clay, and Steve Mitchell. *Idaho Unbound*. Hailey, ID: West Bound Books, 1998.

Robertson, R.G. *Idaho Echoes in Time*. Boise: Tamarack Books, 1998.

Scott, Robert A. *Chief Joseph and the Nez Perces*. New York: Facts on File, 1993.

Fiction

Beatty, Patricia. *Bonanza Girl*. New York: Morrow/Beech Tree Books, 1993.

Boos, Kevin. *The Canyon Door*. Boise: Writer's Press Service, 1994.

Gregory, Kristiana. *Jenny of the Tetons*. San Diego: Harcourt, 1989.

Shipley, Arthur Hayes. *Gray Shadow*. Fresno, CA: Pioneer Publishing, 1979.

VIDEOS

Other Faces, Other Lives: Asian Americans in Idaho. Rocksteady Productions, 1990.

Outdoor Idaho. Boise: Idaho Public Television, 1992.

Portrait of America: Idaho. Raintree Publishing.

Proceeding Through a Beautiful Country: A Television History of Idaho. Boise: Idaho Public Television.

Statehood Day, 1990. Boise: KTVB Television.

Visions of Idaho. 15 episodes. Boise: Idaho Public Television.

CD-ROMS

The Oregon Trail. Minneapolis: MECC, 1993.

U.S. Geography: The Rockies. Dallas: ZCI Publishing, 1994.

WEBSITES

The State of Idaho Home Page is located at www.state.id.us on the World Wide Web. It contains information about Idaho state government and offers hundreds of links to webpages about the state's regions, communities, points of interest, and upcoming events. Two of Idaho's leading newspapers are online at www.idahostatesman.com and www.idahonews.com.

INDEX

Page numbers for charts, graphs, and illustrations are in boldface.

actors, 133
agriculture, 23, 24, 48, **50**, 53, 62–65, **64**, **105**, 125
Albertson, Joe, 128
Alexander, Moses, 56
Andrus, Cecil, 56, **58**
animals, 20, **20**, 21, 31, **105**, 111, **119**, 122, **122**, 135
architecture, 108–109, **109**, 136
art, 128–129, 130, 136

Basques, **65**, 79, **81**, 126, 136
birds, 23, 119, 122, 136
Boise, 44–45, 53, **54–55**, 77, 84, 85, 108–111, **109**, **110**
borders, 12, 14, 75–76, 121
Borglum, Gutzon, 128–129
Bridger, Jim, 36–37
Brink, Carol Ryrie, 92–95, **94**, 129
Bruneau Dunes, 111, **114**
Burroughs, Edgar Rice, 92, **93**, 129
business, 96–98, 125, 128, 132

capital, 44–45, **54–55**, 75–76
central Idaho, **107**, 107–108
"China Polly," 99
Church, Frank, **97**, 98, 129
cities, 23, **51**, 88, 108–111
Clark, William, **34**, 34–35, 92
climate, 17–18, **18**, **19**, 38, 121

Colter, John, 36–37
Corps of Discovery, 34–35, 132
Craters of the Moon, 113, **113**, 136

dams, 24–26, 53
Depression, 48–50
De Smet, Pierre Jean, 37

eastern Idaho, 114–117, **116**, **117**
economy, 25–26, 48–50, **61**, 61–62, 68–70, 125
education, 57, 124
endangered species, **21**, 24–25, 122
energy, 24–26, 52, 53, 109, 124
environment, 22, 25–27, 52, 53, 98–99
ethnicity, 78–79, **80**. *See also* Basques; Native Americans
explorers, 33, **34**, 34–35, 92, 132, 133
extremist groups, 82–83

Farnsworth, Phil, 129, **129**
festivals, 79, **80**, **81**, 84, 85, 87, **87**, 125–128
fires, 17, 48, 49, 124
fish, 24–26, 63–68, 121, 122
Fisher, Vardis, 92, 130
fishing, 70, 115, 135
forests, 18, 19–20, 22, **22**, **69**
Fort Hall, 37, **39**, 134
fossils, 111, 121, 135

Franklin, 39, 41, 123
fur trapping, 35–37, **36**

Gass, Patrick, 35
gems, 68–70, **69**, **119**
geology, 111, 113, **113**, 135
gold, 41, **44**, 70, 111, 123
government
    federal, 57, 83
    state, 56–59, **57**
Green, Emma Edwards, 130

Hells Canyon, 14, **16**, 56, 107, 134
Hemingway, Ernest, 92, 130, **130**
Henry, Andrew, 35–36
hiking, 70, **71**, 108
history, 40–48, 123–124, 136
hot springs, 115–117, 135

industry, 48, 53, 61–62, 68–70, 97–98, 125
inventors, 129, **129**

Japanese Americans, 51–52, **52**, 124
jobs, 61–62, **67**, 68–70
Joseph, Chief, 45–46, **46**, 130–131

Killebrew, Harmon, 131, **131**
Kramer, Jerry, 131

labor unions, 48
lakes, 18, 104, 115, 121
land, 14, 15, **15**, 61–62

legends, 33
Lewis, Meriwether, **34**, 34–35, 41, **44**, 44–45, 92
Lewiston, **24**, 25–26, 44–45, 82–83, 84, 104–105
livestock, 63, **65**

manufacturing, 62, **62**, 125
minerals, 68–70. *See also* gold
mining, 41, 42, 48, **49**, 53, 56, 68–70, 98–99, **112**, 137
missions, 37, 84, 105, 123, 136–137, **137**
Mormons, 38–39, **40**, 76, **77**, 123, 136
mountain men, 35–36, **36**, 84, 126
mountains, 14, **15**, 17, **28–29**, 114–115, 117, 121
museums, 79, 85, 105, 135, 136
music, 84, 85, **86**, 125, 126, 128

name, 41, 119
Nathoy, Lalu, 99
Native Americans, 30–33, **32**, **34**, 35, 37, 45–47, **46**, 59–61, **60**, 79, **80**, 84, 105, 123, 124, 127, 130–131, 132, 134
natural resources, 68–70, **69**, 125
newspapers, 123
northern Idaho, 19–20, 30, 31, 60, 76. *See also* panhandle

O'Brien, Dan, **131**, 131–132
Oregon Trail, 38, **39**, 116–117, 127, **127**, 134
Ostner, Charles, **32**, 109–110

panhandle, 12, **69**, 75–76, 104–105
parks, **15**, 56, 105, 113, 129, 134, 135, 136–137, **137**
pioneers, 37–39, **39**, 41, 99, 135
plains, 15, 23, 63, **65**, **105**
plants, 20, 30, 31, 74, **119**, 122
poets, 92, **93**, 132
politics, 22, 59–61, **97**, 98
population, 23, 47, **51**, 76–78, 79, 86, 88
ports, 104–105, 124
potatoes, 49, **50**, 63, **64**, 65, **65**, 66, 84, 96–98, 127–128, 132, 136
Pound, Ezra, 92, **93**, 132

racism, 82–83, 99
radio stations, 79
railroads, 42, **42**, 49–50, 123
recipe, 66
recreation, **26–27**, 70–71, **71**, 84, 104, 108
religion, 37, 38–39, 76, **77**
River of No Return, 108, 129, 134
rivers, 14–15, **16**, 18, 23, **24**, 24–27, **27**, 34, 63, **107**, 108, 121, 135, 137
roads, 14, 18, 74, 76, 108
rodeos, 84, **85**, 125–126, 127
Rodgers, Sarah, 38

Sacagawea, 132
Schwantes, Carlos A., 44
sculpture, 87, **87**, 109–110, **128**, 128–129
settlers, 38–39, **40**, 123, **132**, 132–133
Shakespeare Festival, 85
shape, 12

Simplot, J. R. "Jack," **96**, 96–98, 132
size, 12, 121
Smith, Edward, **28–29**
snow, 18, **19**, 87, **87**
songs, 43, 120
southern Idaho, 19–20, 30, 76, 92, 108–117
Spalding, Henry and Eliza, 37, 105, 123, **132**, 132–133
sports, 49–50, 84, 87, 100–101, 104, **107**, **131**, 131–132, 133
statehood, 40–48, 119
state seal, 130
Street, Picabo, **100**, 100–101, 133
styles, 74, **75**
Sun Valley, 50, 85, 92, 111–114, **115**, 124, 128, 130, 134, 137
Symms, Steve, 22

technology, 53, 62, **62**
Thompson, David, 35, 133
timber, 48, 53, 68–70, 84, 98–99, 125
tourism, 49–50, 53, 70–71, **71**
tourist sites, 104–117, **106**, **110**, 134–137, **137**
towns, 41, **44**, **82**, **88**, 89, 111, 135, 137
trade, 35–37, **50**, 133, 134
transportation, 74, **75**, 75–76, 108
trees, 19–20, 119, 121–122, 135
Turner, Lana, 133

waterfalls, 111, 134
Weaver, Randy, 83
website, 141
wildlife refuges, 22, 23
World War II, 51
writers, 92–95, **93**, **94**, 129
Wyeth, Nathaniel, 37, **39**